以英文微视频传播中国文化

Communicating Chinese Culture Internationally via English Micro Videos

高琳琳　韩英焕　刘亚梅　金品卓　刘　岩　韩　博　编著

北方联合出版传媒(集团)股份有限公司
万卷出版有限责任公司

图书在版编目（CIP）数据

以英文微视频传播中国文化 / 高琳琳等编著. —沈阳：万卷出版有限责任公司，2023.5
ISBN 978-7-5470-6254-8

Ⅰ.①以… Ⅱ.①高 … Ⅲ.①中华文化—文化传播—英文 Ⅳ.①G125

中国国家版本馆CIP数据核字（2023）第074876号

出版发行：北方联合出版传媒（集团）股份有限公司
　　　　　万卷出版有限责任公司
　　　　　（地址：沈阳市和平区十一纬路29号　邮编：110003）
印　刷　者：辽宁鼎籍数码科技有限公司
幅面尺寸：185mm×260mm
字　　数：280千字
印　　张：15.5
出版时间：2023年5月第1版
印刷时间：2023年5月第1次印刷
责任编辑：高　爽
封面设计：徐春迎
版式设计：李　想
责任校对：张　莹
ISBN 978-7-5470-6254-8
定　　价：68.00元
联系电话：024-23284090
传　　真：024-23284448

序

改革开放以来，随着我国综合国力的持续增强，中国在国际上的影响力不断扩大，正在一步步走近世界舞台的中央。与此同时，中西文化交流态势也正在逐步由"西学东渐"向"东学西传"转变，中国文化正在自信地大踏步走出去。作为一项重大国家战略，中国文化走出去是建设中国特色社会主义文化强国、增强中国文化国际影响力和竞争力的强力引擎。为此，要更好推动中国文化走出去，以文载道、以文传声、以文化人，向世界阐释推介更多具有中国特色、体现中国精神、蕴藏中国智慧的优秀文化。

国际交流与合作是高校的核心职能之一，推动中国文化走出去是高校的职责，更是每个哲学社会科学工作者的使命。习近平总书记在中国人民大学考察时强调，要发挥哲学社会科学在融通中外文化、增进文明交流中的独特作用，传播中国声音、中国理论、中国思想，让世界更好读懂中国，为推动构建人类命运共同体作出积极贡献。总书记还要求哲学社会科学工作者以回答中国之问、世界之问、人民之问、时代之问为学术己任，以彰显中国之路、中国之治、中国之理为思想追求。

中国文化如何创新方式，寻求中国故事的国际表达？如何打破文化差异这道壁垒，从"走出去"到"走进去"？英语是一个沟通中外的重要语言工具，是传播文化的桥梁。《大学英语教学指南（2020版）》明确指出，"大学英语课程可以培养学生对中国文化的理解和阐释能力，服务中国文化对外传播"。然而，常规的大学英语课程或教材承担着培养学生综合英语应用能力、跨文化能力、自主学习能力，以及综合文化素养，因此往往难以帮助学生掌握基础的中国文化知识，系统培养学生用英语传播中国文化的能力。《以英文微视频传播中国文化》可以有效弥补大学英语教学这方面的不足。该书不是一本常规意义上的英文教材，而是一个以英文为载体传播中国文化的"百宝箱"，展示中国文化的"万花筒"。它的直接受众不仅仅是学习大学英语的学生，更包括中国千千万万致力于弘扬中国文化的有志之士，间接受众则是欲了解中国文化的外国人。它可以帮助所有学习者运用新媒体、新技术，以及外国人以更容易接受的形式，以英语母语的思维方式传播中国文化，让外国人感受到中国文化的无穷魅力。

出版一本书，让人人皆可成为中国文化的传播者。可见编者助推中国文化走出去，以传播中国声音、中国理论、中国思想为己任的博大胸怀和殷殷情怀。

向编者致敬！向每一位致力于传播中国文化的有志之士致敬！

2022年7月于南京大学

前　言

"讲好中国故事，传播好中国声音，展示真实、立体、全面的中国"，是2021年以来提升我国国际传播能力的重要国家发展战略之一。外语教育始终肩负着服务于国家发展战略，在不同时期为不同领域培养国际化人才的重任。

以云计算、大数据为代表的智能化时代悄然到来。信息化技术催生出了智能化时代独有的"沉浸"特征，它是新时代建构主流意识形态认同的重要逻辑起点。

21世纪的教育新使命需要培养学习者六个方面的核心竞争力，包括自主学习、语言、辩证思维、文化交流及传播、创新与合作。因此，外语教育要融合语言与思维两方面的能力培养。

《以英文微视频传播中国文化》面向社会各界热衷于用外语传播好中国声音的爱国人士，旨在助力每一位既懂外语又擅长自媒体技术的读者，尤其是青年读者，以增强中国国际认同感为己任，顺应智能化时代发展，坚持传播马克思主义价值观，浸润式润物细无声地向世界宣介中国主张、中国智慧和中国方案，积极助力共同构建人类命运共同体。

在新文科教育理念的引导下，外语教育的跨学科交叉融合发展趋势更加突显。新文科强调"融合"，必须避免两张皮，要在"融合"上有所创新。

教育家杜威指出：所有真正的教育都来自于经验的教育理念，并不意味着一切经验都具有同等的、真实的教育作用；直接经验是增长智慧和发展理性的基础，教育应以学生的直接经验为中心。

依据新文科的融合创新理念和杜威的"直接经验"教育理念，《以英文微视频传播中国文化》致力于为学习者搭建通过质疑、调查、探究等，为真实的全球议题提出中国方案的语言学习"脚手架"。

本书具有如下特色：

一、致力于多学科交叉融合，设计"全球议题"项目式学习语境

《以英文微视频传播中国文化》为避免两张皮，邀请国际传播方向专家和思想政治教育专家协助外语教师，创新融合设计"全球议题"项目式真实学习语境。实践由南京大学王海啸教授及其团队原创的PBLL-C中国特色项目化语言深度学习教育理念。

二、基于大数据，融合线上线下复训"理解性输入"篇章英文句子结构

《以英文微视频传播中国文化》充分利用智能化时代大数据工具，针对著名语言学家王力的精辟观点——英语句子结构上具有后开放性特点，开发学习者自主学习复训题库。

三、立足学习与学力的可视化，采用"成长档案袋"评价

《以英文微视频传播中国文化》着重关注学习过程、提升学习质量及学生自主学习，更强调学习者创作作品获社会评价结果，以实现充分发挥"真实性评价"的价值与能量，培育新时代的"思考者"与"探究者"为目标。更重要的是，依据学习的内涵与过程使学习者发现成就度与项目式学习开展的能力。

章节结构

本册书共4大模块，每个模块主题与知识结构相互关联。具体结构与各部分简介如下：

Module Topic

以问题的形式呈现模块主题，引发学习者对主题的思考。以问题带动思考，促动学习者进一步自主性探究。

Section A

每个模块中的9篇"Interpretive Input"是主体部分，各包含一个英文语篇和复训练习。9个语篇围绕同一主题，从不同角度展现、说明、分析或探讨，培养学习者从多元视角辨析问题的能力。同时训练学习者将所学的话题知识与六个方面的核心竞争力迁移输出到自己的创作产出中。

Structure of Section A

Reading Comprehension

Interpretive Input

解释性语篇输入。首先呈现模块主题某一视角下短小、精练的英文语篇，然后用汉语提供语篇相关背景简介，最后再用英文引出几个辩证思考性问题。

Background Information

汉语背景简介。为增强学习者对英文语篇的宏观理解和学习探究兴趣，尽力减少读者阅读理解英文的倦怠感，特别采用汉语简介。

Critical Thinking

辩证思考性问题。针对36个英文语篇设计紧密相关的思辨性问题，引导读者深入思考，用英文表达观点，培养其六个方面的核心竞争力。

Language Focus

语言知识迁移输出复现、复训。力求培养读者"传播好中国声音"的英文表达自信力，激发其积极加入国际传播矩阵的兴趣，特别采用句子主干、句子附加成分、非谓语动词、句子类型、构词与常用搭配和纵横拼字游戏六大复现、复训相结合的组训模式。

Section B　Module Project

模块项目。学习者围绕由多学科专家融合创新设计的模块项目，完成项目实施方案的构思、设计、制作和产出。

Section C　Learners' Presentation

学习者成果展示。学习者基于模块项目的产出作品通过线上平台发布，获得教师、社会评价，学习者结合评价可以不断完善作品。

Section D　Reflective Assessment

成长档案袋评价。根据学习过程中学习者的一切成长轨迹来设计成长记录评价表，包括线上自学所得机评、创作作品取得的社会评价、学习者探寻"我努力了吗？""我快乐吗？"的自我评价体悟。

CONTENTS

Module One
What Facts of Chinese People Do You Know? 你知道哪些中国人的故事?

Module Two
What Do You Know about Chinese Culture? 你了解多少中国文化?

Module Three
What Will You Do to Facilitate Green Development? 你将如何助力绿色发展？

Module Four
What Changes in China Have You Seen? 中国发生了哪些变化？

Module One

What Facts of Chinese People Do You Know?

你知道哪些中国人的故事？

《*丝缠万里*》画面中年轻的军嫂倚在 "一人参军全家光荣" 的对联下，正在仔细阅读微信上的内容，她的专注与思念的表情，使观众自然联想到远在外地站岗卫疆的丈夫。它承载的重要意义是，人的情感和需要在国家利益面前的选择与坚守。（艺术评论家王健）

  In the painting，the young military spouse is leaning against the Spring Festival Couplet of "one person joins the army and the whole family is glorious"，while carefully reading her message in WeChat. Her facial expression of concentration and missing her husband naturally reminds readers of the husband who is standing guard on frontier. The significance of the painting lies in selfless decision and perseverance when personal emotional needs contradict national interests. (Art critic：WANG Jian)

Section A　Interpretive Input

Chinese Scientists 中国科学家

It is generally recognized that scientists of China are patriotic, dedicated, innovative, collaborative, and eager for seeking truth, which is a priceless treasure to boost national revival. With these powerful and strong mind supports, Chinese scientists have made marvelous achievements in various fields. Undoubtedly, the passed-down invaluable assets will be handed on to those promoted young successive scientists.

Reading Comprehension

Background Information

中国科学家是中华民族的宝贵财富。一代代科技工作人员用智慧和汗水浇灌出中国的崭新面貌，用创新和创造走出一条高水平的科技自立自强之路。面对百年未有之大变局，我们要将科学报国的光荣传统传承下去，坚守追求真理、不畏艰险的科学境界，弘扬敢于创新、求真严谨的学术风气，自觉将个人理想的实现融入国家发展事业中，在科学事业上孜孜不倦，不断探索前沿，不断取得重要科技领域新的突破。

Critical Thinking

Question One：If some scientists have made brilliant achievements, but those are against humanity, how will you judge them?

Question Two：What character traits can you list of a good scientist?

Question Three：Does science need ethics?

Language Focus

英语句子结构上具有后开放性特点，因此在使用英语表达时应该先将句子的主干提取出来，最后再添上句子的其他附加成分。

句子主干 指的是构成一个完整句子的框架，主要包括几个基本句子成分：主语、谓语、宾语、表语。

本语篇一共由3个句子构成，它们的句子主干分别是：

☆ It is recognized.

☆ Scientists have made achievements.

☆ Assets will be handed on.

句子附加成分 句子附加成分指的是去除一个完整句子中的主干部分剩余的修饰、补充说明部分，主要包括几个基本句子成分：定语、状语、宾语补足语、主语补足语、同位语、插入语。

本语篇的句子附加成分如下：

★ generally（副词作状语）

★ that scientists of China are patriotic，dedicated，innovative and collaborative，and eager for seeking truth（it作形式主语，that引导的主语从句作真正主语）

★ which is a priceless treasure to boost national revival（非限定性定语从句）

★ with these powerful and strong mind supports（介词短语作原因状语）

★ Chinese（形容词作定语）

★ marvelous（形容词作定语）

★ in various fields（介词短语作后置定语）

★ undoubtedly（副词作状语）

★ passed-down（复合过去分词作定语）

★ invaluable（形容词作定语）

★ those（指示代词作定语）

★ promoted（过去分词作定语）

★ young（形容词作定语）

★ successive（形容词作定语）

非谓语动词 是指动词在句子中不作谓语时的形式，因此它不受主语的限制。非谓语动词在英语句子中使用频繁且广泛。它可以在句子中充当除了谓语之外的其他成分：主语、宾语、表语、定语、状语、补语等。非谓语动词分为3大类：

◆ 动词不定式：to do / to be

◆ 动名词：doing / being

◆ 分词，一个是现在分词：doing / being；另一个是过去分词：done / been。

本语篇中非谓语动词的使用：

◇ scientists of China are patriotic，dedicated...eager for **seeking** truth 动名词短语作宾语，表示动作的抽象概念化

◇ a priceless treasure **to boost** national revival 动词不定式作后置定语，表用途、将来

◇the **passed-down** invaluable assets 复合过去分词作定语，表示被动、完成

◇those **promoted** young successive scientists 过去分词作定语，表示被动、完成

句子类型 主要包括：简单句、复合句和并列句。在用英文表达时，尽量得体、恰当地交叉使用它们。简单句是指，一个主语或者两个、多个并列主语加上一个谓语或者两个、多个并列谓语构成的句子。复合句是指，一个主句加上一个或者多个从句构成的句子。并列句是指，由并列连词把两个或多个简单句连在一起构成的句子。

本语篇中句子类型的使用：

◎It is generally recognized that scientists of China are patriotic, dedicated, innovative, collaborative, and eager for seeking truth, which is a priceless treasure to boost national revival.

复合句：一个主句 It is generally recognized.

两个从句，从句一是 that scientists of China are patriotic, dedicated, innovative, collaborative, and eager for seeking truth，从句二是 which is a priceless treasure to boost national revival。

◎With these powerful and strong mind supports, Chinese scientists have made marvelous achievements in various fields.

简单句：一个主语 scientists，一个谓语 have made。

◎Undoubtedly, the passed-down invaluable assets will be handed on to those promoted young successive scientists.

简单句：一个主语 assets，一个谓语 will be handed on。

主从复合句点拨：无论是主句还是从句，叫作"句"就一定有谓语动词。从句也是句子，判定是什么从句就看该从句在整个复合句中充当什么句子成分。如，主语从句就是该从句在整个复合句中作主语成分，而这个主语由于太长显得头重脚轻，就用 it 来充当形式上的主语。由 it 作形式主语，that 引导的主语从句作真正的主语在英文表达中使用频率较高。

构词与常用搭配

patriotic（a.）爱国的：由词根 patri=father（家长；祖国）加上形容词后缀 -ic 构成。

常用搭配：patriotic songs，patriotic activities，patriotic sentiments，patriotic feeling

dedicated（*a.*）专注投入的：由词根dic（声称）加上前缀de-（表示"强调"），加上动词后缀-ate，再变为过去分词作形容词用。

常用搭配：dedicated to，dedicated followers，dedicated teachers，dedicated team，dedicated staff

innovative（*a.*）革新的：由词根nov（新）加上前缀in-（表示"加强"），加上形容词后缀-tive构成。

常用搭配：innovative design，innovative thinking， innovative products，innovative idea，innovative method，innovative work

collaborative（*a.*）协作的：由词根labor（劳作）加上表示"强调"的前缀col-，加上形容词后缀-tive构成。

常用搭配：collaborative projects，collaborative studies，collaborative research，collaborative effort，collaborative management

revival（*n.*）复兴：由词根viv=life（生命）加上前缀re-（再，又），再加上名词后缀-al构成。同一个词根变化而来的还有：survival（幸存），前缀sur-（超越）加上词根viv（生命），再加上表示"状态"的名词后缀-al，表示超越一场事故还活着；vivid（生动的）。

常用搭配：the revival of，economic revival，music revival，national revival

marvelous（*a.*）非凡的：由词根mar=mir=wonder/look（惊奇；看），加上形容词后缀-ous构成。

常用搭配：marvelous deeds，marvelous invention，perfectly marvelous，really marvelous，marvelous opportunity，marvelous performance，marvelous time

asset（*n.*）资产：源于拉丁语，原义表示"足够的"，后衍生出"宝贵的人或东西"。

常用搭配：valuable asset，important asset，great asset，intangible asset，financial asset，capital asset

successive（*a.*）接替继承的：由词根cess=go（行走，前进）加上前缀suc-（随后，接着），再加上形容词后缀-ive构成。

常用搭配：successive administrations，successive governments，a successive year，

successive generations

Crossword Puzzle

Across

2. coming or happening one after another in a series

4. feeling a lot of love, respect, and duty towards one's own country

6. extremely enjoyable or exciting

7. to help something to increase, improve, or become more successful

10. people or groups working together to produce something

11. spending all one's time and effort on something

12. new, original, and advanced; incenting or using new ideas, methods, equipment, etc.

Down

1. something is certainly true or is accepted by everyone

3. extremely useful

5. a useful or valuable quality

8. the process of becoming active, successful, or popular again

9. the fact of achieving or succeeding at things in general

Chinese Philosophers 中国哲学家

A large number of Chinese thinkers comparable to the most influential philosophers in the world emerged during the Spring and Autumn Period and the Warring States Period, which are considered as the most flourishing period of Chinese thought and wisdom. There are mainly four schools of philosophy: Confucianism, Taoism, Mohism and Legalism. The main view of Confucianism is benevolence, righteousness, propriety, wisdom and faithfulness; the core ideology of Taoism is "Tao". Some of the representative views of Taoism are to govern by inaction, to follow the rules of nature, to be both rigid and soft and the idea that when something reaches its extreme, its course reverses; the key viewpoint of Mohism is all-embracing love and non-offensive; the point of philosophers of Legalism is to strengthen the army and govern the country by law.

Reading Comprehension

Background Information

公元前800年至公元前200年被一位德国哲学家称作人类文明的"轴心时代"。这一时期，哲学世界出现了影响后世的苏格拉底、柏拉图、琐罗亚斯德、犹太先知和释迦牟尼。同一时期的中国，出现了最为辉煌和璀璨的古代中国哲学思想和文化。当时的诸子百家争鸣盛况空前，因此诞生了诸多对后世影响深远的哲学流派与哲学家。

Critical Thinking

Question One: Under what circumstances did Lao Tzu put forward the idea of governing by inaction? Can it be applied to modern society?

Question Two: Is Mo tsu's idea of all-embracing love too difficult for ordinary people to achieve? How can we achieve all-embracing love?

Question Three: What moral qualities did ancient Chinese philosophers possess?

Language Focus

英语句子结构上具有后开放性特点，因此在使用英语表达时应该先将句子的主干提取出来，最后再添上句子的其他附加成分。

句子主干 指的是构成一个完整句子的框架，主要包括几个基本句子成分：主语、谓语、宾语、表语。

本语篇一共由7个句子构成，它们的句子主干分别是：

☆ Thinkers emerged.

☆ There are schools.

☆ The view is benevolence, righteousness, propriety, wisdom and faithfulness.

☆ The ideology is "Tao".

☆ Views are to govern, to follow, to be and the idea.

☆ The viewpoint is love and non-offensive.

☆ The point is to strengthen.

句子附加成分 指的是去除一个完整句子中的主干部分剩余的修饰、补充说明部分，主要包括几个基本句子成分：定语、状语、宾语补足语、主语补足语、同位语、插入语。

本语篇的句子附加成分如下：

★ A large number of（名词短语作定语）

★ Chinese（形容词作定语）

★ comparable to the most influential philosophers in the world（形容词短语作后置定语）

★ during the Spring and Autumn Period and the Warring States Period（介词短语作时间状语）

★ which is considered as the golden age of Chinese thought and wisdom（非限定性定语从句）

★ mainly（副词作状语）

★ four（数词作定语）

★ of philosophy（介词短语作后置定语）

★ Confucianism, Taoism, Mohism and Legalism（名词作补语）

★ main（形容词作定语）

★ of Confucianism（介词短语作后置定语）

★ core（形容词作定语）

★ of Taoism（介词短语作后置定语）

★ some（限定词作定语）

★ of the representative（介词短语作定语）

★by inaction（介词短语作状语）

★the rules of nature（名词短语作宾语）

★both rigid and soft（名词短语作表语）

★that when a thing reaches its extreme，it reverses its course（that引导从句作idea的同位语，该同位语由句子充当：when引导的条件状语从句，表示对客观情形的陈述）

★key（形容词作定语）

★of Mohism（介词短语作后置定语）

★all-embracing（动名词作定语）

★of philosophers of Legalism（介词短语作后置定语）

★by law（介词短语作状语）

非谓语动词 是指动词在句子中不作谓语时的形式，因此它不受主语的限制。非谓语动词在英语句子中使用频繁且广泛。它可以在句子中充当除了谓语之外的其他成分，主语、宾语、表语、定语、状语、补语等。非谓语动词分为3大类：

◆动词不定式：to do / to be

◆动名词：doing / being

◆分词，一个是现在分词：doing / being；另一个是过去分词：done / been。

本语篇中非谓语动词的使用：

◇**to govern** by inaction，**to follow** the rules of nature，**to be** both rigid and soft 动词不定式短语作表语表观点。

◇**all-embracing** love 动名词作名词love的定语，表示动作概念化、名词的性质与用途。

◇**to strengthen** the army and **govern** the country by law动词不定式短语作表语，用来表达观点。

句子类型 主要包括：简单句、复合句和并列句。在用英文表达时，尽量得体、恰当地交叉使用它们。简单句是指，一个主语或者两个、多个并列主语加上一个谓语或者两个、多个并列谓语构成的句子。复合句是指，一个主句加上一个或者多个从句构成的句子。并列句是指，由并列连词把两个或多个简单句连在一起构成的句子。

本语篇中句子类型的使用：

◎A large number of Chinese thinkers comparable to the most influential philosophers in the world emerged during the Spring and Autumn Period and the Warring States Period, which is considered as the most flourishing period of Chinese thought and wisdom.

复合句：一个主句A large number of Chinese thinkers comparable to the most influential philosophers in the world emerged during the Spring and Autumn Period and the Warring States Period，一个从句 which is considered as the most flourishing period of Chinese thought and wisdom。

◎There are mainly four schools of philosophy: Confucianism, Taoism, Mohism and Legalism.

简单句：there be 句型中一个主语 schools，一个谓语are。

◎The main view of Confucianism is benevolence, righteousness, propriety, wisdom and faithfulness.

简单句：主系表结构，一个主语The view，一个系动词is，并列多个表语 benevolence, righteousness, propriety, wisdom and faithfulness。

◎The core ideology of Taoism is "Tao".

简单句：主系表结构，一个主语The ideology，一个系动词is，一个表语Tao。

◎Some of the representative views of Taoism are to govern by inaction, to follow the rules of nature, to be both rigid and soft and the idea that when a thing reaches its extreme, it course reverses.

简单句：主系表结构，一个主语 views，一个系动词are，多个并列表语to govern, to follow, to be and the idea。

◎the key viewpoint of Mohism is all-embracing love and non-offensive;

简单句：主系表结构，一个主语the viewpoint，一个系动词is，两个并列表语love and non-offensive。

◎the point of philosophers of Legalism is to strengthen the army and govern the country by law.

简单句：主系表结构，一个主语the point，一个系动词is，一个表语to strengthen。

主从复合句点拨：无论是主句还是从句，叫作"句"就一定有谓语动词。从句也是句子，判定是什么从句就看该从句在整个复合句中充当什么句子成分。例如，非限定性定语从句就是该从句在整个复合句中作定语成分，对前面整个主句或者主句的某一部分起到补充说明作用。非限定性定语从句在英文表达中使用频率较高。

构词与常用搭配

comparable（*a.*）比较的：由前缀 com-（共同）加上词根 par（相等），后缀-able（形容词词尾）构成。

常用搭配：comparable to, comparable prices, on comparable basis

philosopher（*n.*）哲学家：源自希腊语，希腊战胜波斯后，希腊出现了一批专门传授辩论和演讲的教师，称为"智者"（sophist），意思就是"有智慧的人"。为了表明自己与这些智者的区别，苏格拉底将自己称为 philosopher（哲学家），意思是"爱智慧的人"。由前缀phil-（爱）加上词根soph（聪明），再加上后缀-er构成。

常用搭配：philosopher king, philosopher-scientist, Greek philosophers

emerge（*v.*）出现：由前缀e-（向外）加上词根merge（浸没）构成。

常用搭配：emerge from sth, emerge in endlessly, emerge one after another

representative（*n.*）代表：由前缀re-（再）加上词根 present（赠送，呈现）和形容词后缀-ative构成。

常用搭配：representative of, representative office, business representative

benevolence（*n.*）仁慈：由前缀 bene-（好）加上词根vol（自愿，意愿）和名词后缀-ence构成。

常用搭配：highest benevolence, term of benevolence, land of benevolence

propriety（*n.*）礼节：由词根proprie=propri（适当的）加上后缀-ty（名词词尾）构成。

常用搭配：propriety disintegration, sense of propriety, not with propriety, propriety standards

ideology（*n.*）思想体系：由词根 ideo=idea（想法）加上名词后缀-logy（学说）构成。后来引申为"思想体系"。

常用搭配：core ideology, guiding ideology, evolution of ideology

reverse（*v.*）转换：由前缀re-（回）加上词根vers（转）构成。

常用搭配：reverse the order, reverse trend, reverse direction, reverse process

offensive（*a.*）攻击的：由前缀of-（对面）加上词根 fens（打击）和形容词后

缀 -ive构成。

常用搭配：offensive team，offensive players，offensive weapons

Crossword Puzzle

Across

2. bring into conformity with rules or principles or usage；impose regulations

4. a wise person who is calm and rational；someone who lives a life of reason with equanimity

5. the state of being inactive

6. include in scope；include as part of something broader；have as one's sphere or territory

9. adhering to moral principles

10. change to the contrary

Down

1. able to be compared or worthy of comparison emerge；come out into view，as from concealment

3. a person who represents others

7. violating or tending to violate or offend against

8. come out into view，as from concealment

Chinese Female Volleyball Athletes 中国女排运动员

It is universally acknowledged that the Chinese female volleyball athletes are synonymous with being tenacious and tough, striving for excellence, never giving up and working together, which has always been inspiring and encouraging countless people. Their positive impact on the nation has gone beyond sporting, motivating people of all social classes and from all walks of life to keep endeavoring. These sport stars will definitely lead the whole society to excellence.

Reading Comprehension

Background Information

中国女排运动员是中国体育的一面旗帜。每逢赛事，女排姑娘们总会成为人们关注的焦点，然而平日艰苦的训练、夜以继日的奋斗，人们并不关注，更不会引来新闻媒体的报道。几十年来一批又一批女排运动员们，坚持不懈、无私奉献、不计回报，塑造出顽强战斗、勇敢拼搏的女排品格与意志。国家的发展离不开这些有着甘于奉献、不怕孤独、勇敢坚韧品格的人们，她们的这些宝贵品质深深鼓舞着中国人民，同时也更需要传承下去、弘扬开来。

Critical Thinking

Question One: What personality traits should competitive athletes have?

Question Two: Do you agree with the idea that professional athletes are affecting our nation's youth?

Question Three: Do you expect to be sound in mind, and sound in body? How to achieve that?

Language Focus

英语句子结构上具有后开放性特点，因此在使用英语表达时应该先将句子的主干提取出来，最后再添上句子的其他附加成分。

句子主干 指的是构成一个完整句子的框架，主要包括几个基本句子成分：主语、谓语、宾语、表语。

本语篇一共由3个句子构成，它们的句子主干分别是：

☆ It is acknowledged.

☆ Impact has gone beyond sporting.

13

☆Stars will lead the society.

句子附加成分 指的是去除一个完整句子中的主干部分剩余的修饰、补充说明部分，主要包括几个基本句子成分：定语、状语、宾语补足语、主语补足语、同位语、插入语。

本语篇的句子附加成分如下：

★universally（副词作状语）

★that the Chinese female volleyball athletes are synonymous with being tenacious and tough, striving for excellence, never giving up and working together（it作形式主语，由 that 引导的主语从句作真正主语）

★being tenacious and tough, striving for excellence, never giving up and working together（由and连接的4个动名词短语作介词with并列宾语）

★which has always been inspiring and encouraging countless people（非限定性定语从句）

★their（物主代词作定语）

★positive（形容词作定语）

★on the nation（介词短语作后置定语）

★motivating people of all social classes and from all walks of life to keep endeavoring（现在分词短语作伴随状语）

★these（指示代词作定语）

★sport（名词作定语）

★definitely（副词作状语）

★whole（形容词作定语）

★to excellence（介词短语作宾语补足语）

非谓语动词 是指动词在句子中不作谓语时的形式，因此它不受主语的限制。非谓语动词在英语句子中使用频繁且广泛。它可以在句子中充当除了谓语之外的其他成分：主语、宾语、表语、定语、状语、补语等。非谓语动词分为3大类：

◆动词不定式：to do/to be

◆动名词：doing/being

◆分词，一个是现在分词：doing/being；另一个是过去分词：done/been。

本语篇中非谓语动词的使用：

◇synonymous with **being tenacious and tough**动名词短语作介词宾语

◇**striving** for excellence动名词短语作介词宾语

◇never **giving** up动名词短语作介词宾语

◇**working** together动名词短语作介词宾语

◇**been inspiring** and **encouraging** countless people现在分词短语作表语

◇has gone beyond **sporting**动名词作介词宾语

◇**motivating** people现在分词短语作伴随状语

◇**to keep** endeavoring动词不定式作宾语补足语

句子类型 主要包括：简单句、复合句和并列句。在用英文表达时，尽量得体、恰当地交叉使用它们。简单句是指，一个主语或者两个、多个并列主语加上一个谓语或者两个、多个并列谓语构成的句子。复合句是指，一个主句加上一个或者多个从句构成的句子。并列句是指，由并列连词把两个或多个简单句连在一起构成的句子。

本语篇中句子类型的使用：

◎It is universally acknowledged that the Chinese female volleyball athletes are synonymous with being tenacious and tough，striving for excellence，never giving up and team working，which has always been inspiring and encouraging countless people.

复合句：一个主句It is universally acknowledged.

两个从句，从句一是that the Chinese female volleyball athletes are synonymous with being tenacious and tough，striving for excellence，never giving up and team working；从句二是which has always been inspiring and encouraging countless people。

◎Their positive impact on the nation has gone beyond sporting，motivating people of all social classes and from all walks of life to keep endeavoring.

简单句：一个主语impact，一个谓语has gone。

◎These sport stars will definitely lead the whole society to excellence.

简单句：一个主语stars，一个谓语will lead。

主从复合句点拨：无论是主句还是从句，叫作"句"就一定有谓语动词。从句也是句子，判定是什么从句就看该从句在整个复合句中充当什么句子成分。例如，定语从句就是该从句在整个复合句中作定语成分。非限定性定语从句在英文表达中使用频率较高；缺少非限定性定语从句也不会影响全句的理解，因为它起补充说明作用，在它的前面往往有逗号与主句隔开。

构词与常用搭配

athlete（*n.*）运动员：源于古希腊词汇表示"奖品；争夺奖品"。后来专门用来指体育竞技赛的选手、健儿。

常用搭配：professional athletes，great athletes，male athletes，women athletes，young athletes

synonymous（*a.*）同义的：由词根nym=name（名字）加上前缀syn-（一起），再加上形容词后缀-ous构成。antonym（反义词）是由同一个词根nym加上前缀anto-=anti-（相反）构成。

常用搭配：synonymous with

tenacious（*a.*）顽强的：由词根ten=hold（握住）加上"有……特征的"形容词后缀-acious构成。

常用搭配：determined and tenacious，tenacious struggle，tenacious belief，tenacious vitality，tenacious qualities，tenacious fighting

inspiring（*a.*）启发灵感的：由词根spir（呼吸）加上前缀in-（进入），再加上形容词后缀-ing（令人……的）构成，意为：吸收活力，即呼入灵感，引申为"鼓舞，启发"。

常用搭配：inspiring story，inspiring experience，inspiring words

encouraging（*a.*）鼓舞人心的：由词根courage（勇气）加上前缀en-=in-（进入），即吸收勇气，再加上形容词后缀-ing（令人……的）构成。

常用搭配：encouraging news，encouraging talk，encouraging and fascinating，encouraging remarks，encouraging comment

impact（*n.*）影响，冲击力：由词根pact（包裹；压紧）加上前缀im-=in-（进入）构成，引申为"影响"。同一个词根构成的还有：compact（压缩），dispacth（分派；派遣）。

常用搭配：impact on，make impact，reduce impact

motivating（*a.*）激励的：由词根mot（移动）加上动词后缀-ate（使……），再加上形容词后缀-ing（令人……的）构成。

常用搭配：motivating factors，motivating forces

endeavor（*n.*）尽力：由词根deavor=debt（债务）源自拉丁语一个表示"义务"的词，加上前缀en-=in-（进入，向内）构成，意即：把一件事当作自己义务去"尽全力"完成。

常用搭配：every endeavor，human endeavor，costly endeavor，collaborative endeavors，endeavor（*v.*）to

Crossword Puzzle

Across

2. strong and able to deal with difficult situations or pain

4. meaning the same or nearly the same

6. stubbornly unyielding

7. to make a lot of effort to achieve something

9. generally accepted，recognized or made known or admitted

10. making people feel enthusiastic or excited about something

12. to try very hard to do something

Down

1. a person trained to compete in sports

3. giving courage or confidence or hope

5. to make someone feel determined to do something or enthusiastic about doing

8. everywhere or in every situation

11. an effect，or an influence

Combating Natural Disasters in China 中国抗击自然灾害

Putting people's lives at the first place has always been the core value of Chinese society. Chinese nation's facts of combating natural disasters have already manifested the long-standing culture which is a good demonstration on collectivism and patriotism. Chinese people are called to respect nature and science, unity and solidarity nationwide, self-sacrifice and a sense of mission for humanity. Chinese people's courage and willpower for tackling disaster risks will definitely promote us to realize the Chinese national rejuvenation and strengthen the building of a modernized socialist country.

Reading Comprehension

Background Information

自然灾害既是对人们发展和生存的挑战，又是对国家品质的洗礼，更是对国家力量的凝聚。中国面对各种自然灾害都会创造人类历史上的英勇壮举，经受住历史大考。中国人在抗击自然灾害的伟大斗争中所展现的坚毅品质，是社会主义核心价值观在新时代最生动的体现，是有效防范各类风险、化解各种挑战，确保不断顺利推进社会主义现代化事业，不断夺取新的伟大胜利、共同创造人类美好未来的宝贵财富。

Critical Thinking

Question One: When facing natural disasters what should people do?

Question Two: What names of natural disaster can you list? Do you know the reasons why natural disasters happen?

Question Three: Do you support the harmonious coexistence between human and nature? What is the inherent relationship between natural disaster and climate changes?

Language Focus

英语句子结构上具有后开放性特点，因此在使用英语表达时应该先将句子的主干提取出来，最后再添上句子的其他附加成分。

句子主干 指的是构成一个完整句子的框架，主要包括几个基本句子成分：主语、谓语、宾语、表语。

本语篇一共由4个句子构成，它们的句子主干分别是：

☆ Putting lives has been the value.

☆Facts have manifested the culture.

☆People are called.

☆Courage and willpower will promote us.

句子附加成分 指的是去除一个完整句子中的主干部分剩余的修饰、补充说明部分，主要包括几个基本句子成分：定语、状语、宾语补足语、主语补足语、同位语、插入语。

本语篇的句子附加成分如下：

★people's（名词所有格作定语）

★at the first place（介词短语作状语）

★always（频度副词作状语）

★core（形容词作定语）

★of Chinese society（介词短语作后置定语）

★Chinese nation's（名词短语作定语）

★of combating natural disasters（介词短语作后置定语）

★already（副词作状语）

★long-standing（形容词作定语）

★which is a good demonstration on collectivism and patriotism（限定性定语从句）

★Chinese（形容词作定语）

★to respect nature and science（动词不定式作主语补足语）

★unity and solidarity nationwide，self-sacrifice and a sense of mission（由and连接的名词短语与第一组名词短语nature and science一起构成动词respect的并列宾语）

★for humanity（介词短语作后置定语）

★Chinese people's（名词短语作定语）

★for tackling disaster risks（介词短语作后置定语）

★definitely（副词作状语）

★to realize the Chinese national rejuvenation（动词不定式作宾语补足语）

★and strengthen the building（由and连接的动词短语作并列宾语补足语）

★of a modernized socialist country（介词短语作后置定语）

非谓语动词 是指动词在句子中不作谓语时的形式，因此它不受主语的限制。非谓语动词在英语句子中使用频繁且广泛。它可以在句子中充当除了谓语之外的其他成分：主语、宾语、表语、定语、状语、补语等。非谓语动词分为3大类：

◆动词不定式：to do / to be

◆动名词：doing / being

◆分词，一个是现在分词：doing / being；另一个是过去分词：done / been。

本语篇中非谓语动词的使用：

◇**Putting people's lives** at the first place动名词短语作主语，表示动作的概念化。

◇facts of **combating natural disasters**动名词短语作介词of宾语，表示动作的概念化。

◇manifested the **long-standing culture**由复合现在分词演变为形容词作定语，表示主动、进行。

◇**to respect** nature and science动词不定式作主语补足语，补充说明主语的具体动作。

◇courage and willpower for **tackling disaster risks**动名词短语作介词for的宾语，表示动作的概念化。

◇promote us **to realize the Chinese national rejuvenation**动词不定式作宾语补足语，补充说明宾语us的具体动作。

◇strengthen the **building of a modernized socialist country**动名词短语作宾语，表示动作的概念化。

句子类型 主要包括：简单句、复合句和并列句。在用英文表达时，尽量得体、恰当地交叉使用它们。简单句是指，一个主语或者两个、多个并列主语加上一个谓语或者两个、多个并列谓语构成的句子。复合句是指，一个主句加上一个或者多个从句构成的句子。并列句是指，由并列连词把两个或多个简单句连在一起构成的句子。

本语篇中句子类型的使用：

◎Putting people's lives at the first place has always been the core value of Chinese society.

简单句：一个主语putting lives，一个谓语has been。

◎Chinese nation's facts of combating natural disasters have already manifested the long-standing culture which is a good demonstration on collectivism and patriotism.

复合句：一个主句Chinese nation's facts of combating natural disasters have already manifested the long-standing culture，一个从句which is a good demonstration on collectivism and patriotism。

◎Chinese people are called to respect nature and science，unity and solidarity nationwide，self-sacrifice and a sense of mission for humanity.

简单句：一个主语people，一个谓语are called。

◎Chinese people's courage and willpower for tackling disaster risks will definitely promote us to realize the Chinese national rejuvenation and strengthen the building of a modernized socialist country.

简单句：两个由and连接的并列主语courage和willpower；一个谓语will promote。

简单句点拨：简单句的句子特征是只有一套主谓结构，它的主语可以由两个或两个以上并列主语构成；谓语也可以由两个或两个以上并列谓语构成。"一套主谓"结构不是一个主语、谓语的同义词。

构词与常用搭配

combat（*v.*）抗击，搏斗：由词根bat=beat（击打）加上前缀com-=together（一起）构成。

常用搭配：combat virus，combat disease，combat inflation，combat unemployment

disaster（*n.*）灾难：由词根aster=star加上表示否定的前缀dis-构成，由原义"不正常星位"引申为"天灾"等含义。

常用搭配：natural disaster，disaster risk，terrible disaster，major disaster，avoid disaster

manifest（*v.*）显示，表明：由词根fest=struck（击打）加上前缀mani-=with hand引申来的"用手击打"即可以清清楚楚感觉到的"显露、显示，表明"。

常用搭配：actions manifest，manifest desire，results manifest，analysis manifests

demonstration（*n.*）证明，展示：由动词demonstrate加名词后缀-ion构成。前缀de-表示"强调"，词根mon是"展示"之意，又如：monitor（监控，检查；显示屏）。

常用搭配：a peaceful demonstration，a violent demonstration，a public demonstration，a mass demonstration，hold/go on/take part in a demonstration

collectivism（*n.*）集体主义：由动词collect（收集，集中）加上名词后缀-ism（主义）构成。

常用搭配：collectivism values，collectivism spirit，collectivism culture，individualism and collectivism，collectivism and socialism

patriotism（*n.*）爱国主义：由词根patri=father，加上名词后缀-ism（主义）构成。

常用搭配：patriotism spirit，real patriotism，true patriotism

unity（*n.*）团结一致；统一体：由词根uni-=one，加上名词后缀-ty构成。

常用搭配：achieve unity，complete unity，safeguard unity，strengthen unity，national unity，European economic unity

solidarity（*n.*）团结：由形容词solid（固体的，坚固的），加上名词后缀-arity构成。

常用搭配：ethnic solidarity，reinforce solidarity，solidarity with，community solidarity

sacrifice（*v.*）牺牲；贡献：由词根 fice=fact（做，从事），加上前缀sacr-（神圣的）构成，原本是指向神贡奉祭品，现代文明社会中其含义引申为"贡献，奉献；为正义事业牺牲、献身"。

常用搭配：make sacrifice，great sacrifice，final sacrifice，ultimate sacrifice，supreme sacrifice，personal sacrifice

humanity（*n.*）人性：由形容词human（人的），加上名词后缀-ity构成。

常用搭配：against humanity，common humanity，a vast sea of humanity，humanities and social sciences，humanities education

promote（*v.*）促进，推动：由词根mot=move（移动）加上前缀pro-（向前）

常用搭配：promote development，promote growth，promote sales，promote reform，promote cooperation

Crossword Puzzle

Across

4. a political theory that the people should own the means of production

7. to show something clearly, especially a feeling, an attitude or a quality

8. the act of not allowing yourself to have or do something in order to help other people

9. people in general

10. love of country and willingness to sacrifice for it

11. to help somebody to happen or develop

12. to do something in order to try to stop something bad from happening or a bad situation from becoming worse

Down

1. an event that proves a face

2. having existed for a long time

3. an unexpected event that kills a lot of people or causes a lot of damage

5. the quality of being united into one

6. the phenomenon of vitality and freshness being restored

8. support by one person or group of people for another because they share feelings, opinions, aims, etc

Online Teachers in China 中国线上教师

China's online education has been booming these years. Online teachers in China are benefiting from the country's intimate relation with the Internet platforms which help them produce, distribute, and also make money from the contents. Online teachers and instructors making a living through Internet-enabled platforms are gradually becoming one of the faces of China's evolving education system thanks to digital economy.

Reading Comprehension

Background Information

互联网的力量使得在线教师在中国获得了极大的认可。在线教师通过网络以直播的方式向学生授课、解惑，超越了时空的限制。网红教师享有近乎名人的地位，并挑战着公众对传统教育的看法。在线教师人数不断增加意味着在当今数字时代的中国，每个人都可以成为导师；同时，随着行业的发展，在线教师的学历是争议的焦点，如何开展网课互动从而提升在线教学效果，如何创新、开发更多实用网络资源和平台等等都是在线教师面临的更大挑战。数字经济使得中国的在线教师群体正在受益于中国与互联网的密切关系。

Critical Thinking

Question One: What are the pros and cons of online teaching?

Question Two: How much do you know about MOOCs, online celebrity teachers, online and offline blended learning and teaching, etc.? Are you a fan of them? Why?

Question Three: Should online education system be applied to public schools?

Language Focus

英语句子结构上具有后开放性特点，因此在使用英语表达时应该先将句子的主干提取出来，最后再添上句子的其他附加成分。

句子主干 指的是构成一个完整句子的框架，主要包括主语、谓语、宾语、表语等基本成分。

本语篇一共由3个句子构成，它们的句子主干分别是：

☆Education has been booming.

☆Teachers are benefiting.

☆Teachers and instructors are becoming one.

句子附加成分 指的是去除一个完整句子中的主干部分剩余的修饰、补充说明部分，主要包括定语、状语、宾语补足语、主语补足语、同位语、插入语等附加成分。

本语篇的句子附加成分如下：

★China's（名词所有格作定语）

★online（形容词作定语）

★these years（名词短语作时间状语）

★in China（介词短语作后置定语）

★the country's（名词所有格作定语）

★intimate（形容词作定语）

★with the Internet platforms（介词短语作后置定语）

★which help them produce，distribute，and also make money（定语从句作后置定语）

★from the contents（介词短语作状语）

★making a living（现在分词作定语）

★through Internet-enabled platforms（介词短语作状语）

★gradually（副词作状语）

★of the faces（介词短语作后置定语）

★of education system（介词短语作后置定语）

★evolving（现在分词作定语）

★thanks to economy（介词短语作原因状语）

★digital（形容词作定语）

非谓语动词 是指动词形式有一定的变换，在句子中不作谓语，因此它不受主语的限制。非谓语动词在英语中很常见。它可以在句子中充当主语、宾语、表语、定语、状语、补语等句子成分。非谓语动词有以下三种形式：

◆动词不定式：to do/to be

◆动名词：doing/being

◆分词，一个是现在分词：doing/being；另一个是过去分词：done/been。

本语篇中非谓语动词的使用：

◇**making a living**现在分词作定语，表示的含义有主动、进行。

◇**evolving** education system现在分词作定语，表示的含义有主动、进行。

句子类型 主要包括简单句、复合句和并列句。在用英文表达时，尽量得体、恰当地交叉使用它们。简单句是指，一个主语或者两个以上主语加上一个谓语或者两个以上谓语构成的句子。复合句是指，一个主句加上一个或者多个从句构成的句子。并列句是指，两个以上简单句由并列连词连在一起构成的句子。

本语篇中句子类型的使用：

◎China's online education has been booming in recent years.

简单句：一个主语China's online education，一个谓语has been booming。

◎Online teachers and instructors making a living through Internet-enabled platforms are gradually becoming one of the faces of China's evolving education system thanks to digital economy.

简单句：一个主语Online teachers and instructors，一个谓语are gradually becoming，一个宾语one of the faces。

◎Online teachers in China are benefiting from the country's intimate relation with the Internet platforms which help them produce, distribute, and also make money from the contents.

复合句：一个主句 Online teachers in China are benefiting from the country's intimate relation with the Internet platforms，一个从句which help them produce, distribute, and also make money from the contents。

主从复合句点拨：从句在整个复合句中充当什么句子成分它就是什么从句。例如，从句作定语它就是定语从句。无论是限定性定语从句还是非限定性定语从句，它们在英文表达中使用频率都很高。

构词与常用搭配

boom（*v.*）迅速发展：它是一个拟声词，原本模拟昆虫群发出的声音，因发展快发出的声音类似昆虫群发出的，后引申为"蓬勃、迅猛发展"。它的同源词还有bomb（爆炸），booming（繁盛的）

常用搭配：economic boom, travel boom, boom years

benefit（*v.*）得益：由bene-好+fit=-fac（做，作）构成。

常用搭配：benefit from，mutual benefit，little benefit，get / gain / obtain benefit

intimate（*a.*）亲密的：由in（在……里）+-tim最高级+ate形容词后缀构成。

常用搭配：intimate relationships，intimate atmosphere

platform（*n.*）平台：源自一个古法语词plat（平的）加上动词 form（形成）而构成的复合词。

常用搭配：an oil / gas platform，launch platform，viewing platform

produce（*v.*）制造：由词根duc（引导）加上前缀pro-（前）构成。

常用搭配：produce result，produce effect，automatically produce，produce seeds，farm produce（*n.*），local produce（*n.*）

evolve（*v.*）（使）逐步发展：由词根volv（卷动）加上前缀e-（向上）构成。

常用搭配：evolve from，evolve into

distribute（*v.*）分发：由词根tribut（交给）加上前缀dis-（分离，分开）构成。

常用搭配：distribute leaflets，distribute materials，distribute food

instructor（*n.*）指导者：由词根struct（建设，结构）加上前缀in-（入，向内），再加上表示"人"的名词后缀 -or构成。

常用搭配：a driving / skiing / swimming / history / science instructor

gradually（*ad.*）逐步地：由词根grad（步，级）加上形容词词缀-ual，再加上副词后缀-ly构成。

常用搭配：gradually improved，gradually spreading

digital（*a.*）数字的：源于词根digit，一个拉丁语词"手指、脚趾"，又因为人们常用手指数数，后引申用来指"个位数"；再加上形容词后缀-al构成。

常用搭配：digital data / age / camera

Crossword Puzzle

Across

3. to develop gradually, or to cause something or someone to develop gradually

4. to give something out to several people, or to spread or supply something

9. slowly over a period of time or a distance

10. recording or storing information as series of the numbers 1 and 0, to show that a signal is present or absent

Down

1. to increase or become successful and produce a lot of money very quickly

2. to be helped by something or to help someone

5. having, or being likely to cause, a very close friendship or personal or sexual relationship

6. a teacher of a college or university subject

7. an opportunity to make your ideas or beliefs known publicly

8. to result in or discover something, especially proof

Good Samaritan in China 中国好人

There lived a man called "Hao Ren", meaning a good Samaritan, near a lake in a village of Shandong Province in eastern China. Over a few decades, the good Samaritan has saved 16 persons' lives, which include a child and a woman. When the kid slipped into the lake by accident, Hao Ren was walking past it and then he risked his safety to dive into the water for getting the drowning child ashore finally. The woman had attempted to commit suicide in the lake, but fortunately she was rescued by Hao Ren. Because he fully recognized the importance of team work and the limitation of his own ability, the good Samaritan organized a rescue team center with volunteers skillful in swimming. Hao Ren has been bestowed the Awards of the National Ethical Model for his "brave action for a just cause". The good Samaritan traits have always been the core value of society for millennia in China.

Reading Comprehension

Background Information

见义勇为是我们的传统美德，每一位见义勇为的英雄身上总有一种力量和品质激励着我们。他们面对不法犯罪分子时，扶正祛邪、大义凛然，在生死关头冲在了人民群众前面，作出了英勇的壮举；他们面对突发的自然灾害事故时，舍生忘我、救死扶伤、临危不惧，在危急时刻展现出大勇大智；他们面对患难群众时，扶危济困、崇德尚善，在危难之中奉献了人间大爱。他们是人民利益的忠实守护者，是人民的英雄、社会的榜样。

Critical Thinking

Question One: Are you willing to be a Good Samaritan within your means?

Question Two: What character traits can you list of good people?

Question Three: Do you agree with this statement—Good deeds have the double benefit of helping the intended recipient and making the doer feel good, as well ?

Language Focus

英语句子结构上具有后开放性特点，因此在使用英语表达时应该先将句子的主干提取出来，最后再添上句子的其他附加成分。

句子主干 指的是构成一个完整句子的框架，主要包括几个基本句子成分：主语、谓语、宾语、表语。

本语篇一共由7个句子构成，它们的句子主干分别是：

☆There lived a man.

☆The good Samaritan has saved lives.

☆Hao Ren was walking and he risked safety.

☆The woman had attempted to commit suicide，but she was rescued.

☆The good Samaritan organized a center.

☆Hao Ren has been bestowed.

☆The traits have been the value.

句子附加成分 指的是去除一个完整句子中的主干部分剩余的修饰、补充说明部分，主要包括几个基本句子成分：定语、状语、宾语补足语、主语补足语、同位语、插入语。

本语篇的句子附加成分如下：

★called "Hao Ren"（过去分词短语作后置定语）

★meaning a good Samaritan（现在分词短语作插入语）

★near a lake in a village of Shandong Province in eastern China（介词短语作there be 句型中的地点状语）

★Over a few decades（介词短语作时间状语）

★16 persons'（名词短语作定语）

★which include a child and a woman（非限定性定语从句）

★When the kid slipped into the lake by accident（时间状语从句）

★past it（介词短语作状语）

★his（物主代词作定语）

★to dive into the water for getting the drowning child ashore finally（动词不定式短语作目的状语）

★in the lake（介词短语作地点状语）

★fortunately（副词作状语）

★by Hao Ren（由介词by引导的介词短语在被动语态句子中引出施动者）

★Because he fully recognized the importance of team work and the limitation of his own ability（原因状语从句中由and连接两个并列宾语）

★with volunteers skillful in swimming（介词短语作后置定语）

★the Awards of the National Ethical Model（名词短语作宾语）

★for his "brave action for a just cause"（介词短语作原因状语）

★the good Samaritan（名词短语作定语）

★always（频度副词作状语）

★core（形容词作定语）

★of society（介词短语作后置定语）

★for millennia（介词短语作时间状语）

★in China（介词短语作地点状语）

非谓语动词 是指动词在句子中不作谓语时的形式，因此它不受主语的限制。非谓语动词在英语句子中使用频繁且广泛。它可以在句子中充当除了谓语之外的其他成分，主语、宾语、表语、定语、状语、补语等。非谓语动词分为3大类：

◆动词不定式：to do / to be

◆动名词：doing / being

◆分词，一个是现在分词：doing / being；另一个是过去分词：done / been。

本语篇中非谓语动词的使用：

◇a man **called** "Hao Ren"过去分词作定语表示的含义有被动、完成。

◇**meaning** a good Samaritan现在分词作插入语表示的含义有伴随。

◇**to dive** into the water动词不定式短语作状语表目的。

◇for **getting** the **drowning** child ashore动名词作介词for宾语，现在分词作定语表示动作的含义有"正在，进行"。

◇attempted **to commit** suicide动词不定式短语作宾语表计划。

◇volunteers skillful in **swimming**动名词作介词in宾语，表示动作概念化。

句子类型 主要包括：简单句、复合句和并列句。在用英文表达时，尽量得体、恰当地交叉使用它们。简单句是指，一个主语或者两个、多个并列主语加上一个谓语或者两个、多个并列谓语构成的句子。复合句是指，一个主句加上一个或者多个从句构成的句子。并列句是指，由并列连词把两个或多个简单句连在一起构成的句子。

本语篇中句子类型的使用：

◎There lived a man called "Hao Ren", meaning a good Samaritan, near a lake in a village of Shandong Province in eastern China.

简单句：there be 句型中一个主语a man，一个谓语lived。

◎Over a few decades, the good Samaritan has saved 16 persons' lives, which include a child and a woman.

复合句：一个主句Over a few decades, the good Samaritan has saved 16 persons' lives，一个从句which include a child and a woman。

◎When the kid slipped into the lake by accident, Hao Ren was walking past it and then he risked his safety to dive into the water for getting the drowning child ashore finally.

复合句：一个主句Hao Ren was walking past it and risked his safety to dive into the water for getting the drowning child ashore finally，一个从句When the kid slipped into the lake by accident。

◎The woman had attempted to commit suicide in the lake, but fortunately she was rescued by Hao Ren.

并列句：由并列连词but把两个简单句The woman had attempted to commit suicide in the lake和fortunately she was rescued by Hao Ren连在一起。

◎Because he fully recognized the importance of team work and the limitation of his own ability, the good Samaritan organized a rescue team center with volunteers skillful in swimming.

复合句：一个主句the good Samaritan organized a rescue team center with volunteers skillful in swimming，一个从句Because he fully recognized the importance of team work and the limitation of his own ability。

◎Hao Ren has been bestowed the Awards of the National Ethical Model for his "brave action for a just cause".

简单句：一个主语Hao Ren，一个谓语has been bestowed。

◎The good Samaritan traits have always been the core value of society for millennia in China.

简单句：一个主语traits，一个谓语have been。

主从复合句点拨：无论是主句还是从句，叫作"句"就一定有谓语动词。从句也是句子，判定是什么从句就看该从句在整个复合句中充当什么句子成分。如，状语从句就是该从句在整个复合句中作状语成分。状语从句在英文表达中使用频率较高，它还可以根据语意、与主句的逻辑关系细分为：时间状语从句、地点状语从句、目的状语从句、原因状语从句、结果状语从句、伴随状语从句等。

构词与常用搭配

Samaritan（*n.*）好心人：该词本义是"撒玛利亚人"，源自《圣经》中一个故事，危难之际在众多过路人中只有Samaritan乐善好施，因此Samaritan一词成了"好心人"的代名词。

常用搭配：a good Samaritan

decade（*n.*）十年期：源自希腊语，词根dec=ten。

常用搭配：the last decade，the past decade，next decade

slip（*v.*）滑落：与slide，slop，slip，slot等同源，最初源自原始印欧语。

常用搭配：slip away，slip over，slip into

ashore（*adv.*）向岸上：由前缀a-（在……的）加上shore（*n.*岸上）构成副词；同类变化有：alone，aloud，aside，away，

常用搭配：wash ashore，go ashore，come ashore，swim ashore

commit（*v.*）做错事：由词根mit=send（派送）加上表示强调的前缀com-构成。该词有贬义色彩，经常和表示负面的名词连用。

常用搭配：commit suicide，commit crime，commit sin

suicide（*n.*）自杀行为：由词根cide=cut=kill，加上前缀sui-=self构成，同类有pesticide（杀虫剂，pest害虫+cide），herbicide（除草剂，herb草本+cide）

常用搭配：attampt suicide，commit suicide，consider suicide，mass suicide，political suicide

bestow（*v.*）授予：由前缀be-表示强调，加上词根stow（把……放好）构成，表示郑重地授予荣誉、称号。

常用搭配：bestow upon，bestow a title，bestow a gift，bestow the awards

cause（*n.*）事业；理由：由词根caus=reason衍生来的。同词根的：because，accuse，excuse

常用搭配：common cause，good cause，just cause，major cause，main cause，primary cause

trait（*n.*）显著特点：与tract同一含义，表示"引，牵拉"，引申为"人的个性；特点"。

常用搭配：a human trait，character traits，personality traits，a positive trait，common trait

millennium（*n.*）一千年：由前缀mil-（千），加上词根enn=year（年）构成。mil=mile是古罗马时期人步行一千步之意。millennium的复数是millennia。

常用搭配：new millenium，a millenium baby，a millenium bug

Crossword Puzzle

Across

2. to save somebody or something from a dangerous or harmful situation

3. to do something illegal or morally wrong

6. a period of 10 years

7. a period of 1000 years

10. the choicest or most essential or most vital part of some idea or experience

11. an organization or idea that people support or fight for

12. your feet slide accidentally and you lose your balance or fall over

Down

1. towards, onto or on land, having come from an area of water such as the sea or a river

4. a person who voluntarily offers help or sympathy in times of trouble

5. the action of deliberately killing yourself

8. connected with beliefs and principles about what is right and wrong

9. to give something to somebody, especially to show how much they are respected

The Westward Relocation of Jiao Tong University 交通大学西迁

In order to boost socialist development, the decision on moving part of Shanghai Jiao Tong University from Shanghai, a coastal city which is internationalized and modernized, to Xi'an, an inland city with ancient civilization, was made in 1955. The faculty of Shanghai Jiao Tong University has perfectly fulfilled the mission. With selfless contributions and pioneering work, they put the national interest at the first and foremost place, which carried on the nation's traditional virtue. The valuable and noble quality will promote Chinese national rejuvenation without doubt.

Reading Comprehension

Background Information

今日的西安交通大学与上海交通大学是同根同源的。1955年，交通大学开始从上海迁至西安，历经四年搬迁工作结束，至此我国有了西安交通大学和上海交通大学两所交通大学。当年交大一大批来自工业、交通、基建、财贸、文教、卫生、军工等行业的"西迁人"扎根关中平原、秦巴深处，为西部发展和国家建设贡献力量和智慧。如今的西安交通大学，不仅是重要的智力库和人才库，更是西部地区改革发展位居前列的科教高地。这一切，都离不开那一场浩浩荡荡的西迁，更离不开交大人宝贵品质的传承与弘扬。

Critical Thinking

Question One: In most cases, which will you choose between individual and national interests? Why?

Question Two: Do you agree with "only when there is a nation, can there be a home"? Why or why not?

Question Three: Are you willing to participate in the Western Development Strategy in China, and make your contributions with passions?

Language Focus

英语句子结构上具有后开放性特点，因此在使用英语表达时应该先将句子的主干提取出来，最后再添上句子的其他附加成分。

句子主干 指的是构成一个完整句子的框架，主要包括几个基本句子成分：主语、谓语、宾语、表语。

本语篇一共由4个句子构成，它们的句子主干分别是：

☆The decision was made.

☆The faculty has fulfilled the mission.

☆They put the interest.

☆The quality will promote rejuvenation.

句子附加成分 指的是去除一个完整句子中的主干部分剩余的修饰、补充说明部分，主要包括几个基本句子成分：定语、状语、宾语补足语、主语补足语、同位语、插入语。

本语篇的句子附加成分如下：

★In order to boost socialist development（介词短语作目的状语）

★on moving part of Shanghai Jiao Tong University from Shanghai to Xi'an（介词短语作后置定语）

★a coastal city（名词短语作同位语）

★which is internationalized and modernized（限定性定语从句）

★an inland city（名词短语作同位语）

★with ancient civilization（介词短语作后置定语）

★in 1955（介词短语作时间状语）

★of Shanghai Jiao Tong University（介词短语作后置定语）

★With selfless contributions and pioneering work（介词短语作伴随状语）

★at the first and foremost place（介词短语作状语）

★which carried on the nation's traditional virtue（非限定性定语从句）

★perfectly（程度副词作状语）

★valuable and noble（形容词性短语作定语）

★Chinese national（形容词性短语作定语）

★without doubt（介词短语作方式状语）

非谓语动词 是指动词在句子中不作谓语时的形式，因此它不受主语的限制。非谓语动词在英语句子中使用频繁且广泛。它可以在句子中充当除了谓语之外的其他成分，主语、宾语、表语、定语、状语、补语等。非谓语动词分为3大类：

◆动词不定式：to do/to be

◆动名词：doing/being

◆分词，一个是现在分词：doing/being；另一个是过去分词：done/been。

本语篇中非谓语动词的使用：

◇the decision on moving part of Shanghai Jiao Tong University from Shanghai 动名词短语作介词on的宾语，表示动作的抽象概念化。

◇**pioneering** work 现在分词作定语表示的含义有主动、进行。

句子类型 主要包括：简单句、复合句和并列句。在用英文表达时，尽量得体、恰当地交叉使用它们。简单句是指，一个主语或者两个、多个并列主语加上一个谓语或者两个、多个并列谓语构成的句子。复合句是指，一个主句加上一个或者多个从句构成的句子。并列句是指，由并列连词把两个或多个简单句连在一起构成的句子。

本语篇中句子类型的使用：

◎In order to boost socialist development, the decision on moving part of Shanghai Jiao Tong University from Shanghai, a coastal city which is internationalized and modernized, to Xi'an, an inland city with ancient civilization, was made by Chinese national government in 1955.

复合句：一个主句the decision on moving part of Shanghai Jiao Tong University from Shanghai to Xi'an was made by Chinese national government in 1955，一个限定性定语从句which is internationalized and modernized。

◎The faculty of Shanghai Jiao Tong University has perfectly fulfilled the mission.

简单句：一个主语The faculty，一个谓语has perfectly fulfilled。

◎With selfless contributions and pioneering work, they put the national interest at the first and foremost place, which carried on the nation's traditional virtue.

复合句：一个主句they put the national interest at the first and foremost place，一个非限定性定语从句which carried on the nation's traditional virtue。

◎The valuable and noble quality will promote Chinese national rejuvenation without doubt.

简单句：一个主语quality，一个谓语will promote。

主从复合句点拨：无论是主句还是从句，叫作"句"就一定有谓语动词。从句也是句子，判定是什么从句就看该从句在整个复合句中充当什么句子成分。如，定语从句就是该从句在整个复合句中作定语成分，它又细分为限定性和非限定性两种。限定性定语从句在语意上不可少，起到修饰先行词的作用；非限定性定语从句即使省略也不影响主句的语意完整性。

构词与常用搭配

coastal（*a.*）沿海的：由名词coast（海岸）加上形容词后缀-al构成。

常用搭配：coastal defence, a coastal city, a coastal road, a coastal town, coastal areas, coastal regions, coastal districts

civilization（*n.*）文明：由形容词civil（市民的）加上表示"……化"的名词后缀-zation构成。同类变化还有：internationalization（国际化），modernization（现代化），等。

常用搭配：ancient civilization, early civilization, alien civilization

faculty（*n.*）全体教师：由动词词根fac（做）加上名词后缀-ty构成，表示做事的能力和才能，后来引申为全体教员。factory（工厂）也是同一个词根fac（做）派生的。

常用搭配：faculty members, English faculty, mathematics faculty

authority（*n.*）当局，权威：由名词author（创作者）加上表示"状态、性质"的名词后缀-ity构成。类似变化还有：由形容词opportune（恰好、碰巧的）加上-ity变成opportunity（机会），由形容词familiar（熟悉的）加上-ity变成familiarity（精通；亲密），等。

常用搭配：Chinese authority, legal authority, supreme authority

academic（*a.*）学术的；理论的：由名词academy（学院）加上形容词后缀-ic构成。

常用搭配：academic year, academic research, academic journal, academic background, academic study

contribution（*n.*）贡献：由动词contribute（捐献）加上名词后缀-ion构成。动词contribute是由表示"给"的词根tribute加上前缀con-（一起together）演变来的。

常用搭配：contribution to, contribution towards, important contribution, valuable contribution, substantial contribution, great contribution

pioneering（*a.*）开拓性的：由名词pioneer加上-ing构成分词作形容词用。名词pioneer源自法语词"步兵"，引申为"先锋，先驱"。

常用搭配：pioneering work, pioneering spirit, pioneering days

foremost（*a.*）最初，首要的：由古代英语演变来的firstest之意，是双重最高级。

常用搭配：foremost concern，foremost authority，foremost scholars

rejuvenation（*n.*）复兴：由形容词young（年轻的）加上表示"再，又"的前缀re-，和动词后缀-ate，再加上名词后缀-ion构成。

常用搭配：rapid rejuvenation，national rejuvenation，great rejuvenation

Crossword Puzzle

Across

2. all the teachers of a particular university or college

5. an official organization or government department that has the power to make decisions

6. an action or a service that helps to cause or increase something

7. introducing ideas and methods that have never been used before

10. to make something increase, or become better or more successful

11. behaviour or attitudes that show high moral standards

12. the phenomenon of vitality and freshness being restored

13. an important official job that a person or group of people is given to do

Down

1. it is used to describe things that relate to the work done in schools, colleges, and universities

3. on land beside an ocean

4. a state of human society that is very developed and organized

8. having fine personal qualities that people admire, such as courage and honesty

9. the most important or famous

Senior Citizens in China 中国老年人

In China, with the increase in ageing population, senior citizens are eager to learn more. The first Senior Citizens' University (SCU) was founded in east China's Shandong Province in 1983. At this kind of special universities, students are free from academic pressure and employment anxiety, and the curriculum is extensive, offering foreign languages, computer skills, music, dance, photography, painting and other crafts, sports and cooking. Many Chinese SCUs offer not only courses in traditional Chinese calligraphy, painting, literature and science, but in snooker, digital graphic design and video editing as well. More SCUs will be set up to ensure senior citizens a fulfilling life. Besides education, senior citizens also need things like elderly care and medical care.

Reading Comprehension

Background Information

中国综合国力逐步增强，中国当代老年人的生活也日益丰富、充实起来。越来越多的老年人注重培养自己的兴趣爱好，并且希望通过增长知识、学习技能和展现才能来融入当今社会、活到老学到老。因此，一大批老年大学在各个地区建立和发展兴盛起来。老人们在老年大学里不仅学习新的知识和技能，健身娱乐的同时还能广交朋友、开发智力。更重要的是，老年人的权益还受到了更多的重视，全社会都对老年人群体倍加关心和理解。

Critical Thinking

Question One: How can the large group of senior citizens be taken good care of when population ageing has come to Chinese society? Which is a better solution for elderly care, home-based, nursing home or tourism endowment?

Question Two: Do you agree with the Chinese old sayings, raising children to prevent from the loneliness and helplessness in old age? Why or why not?

Question Three: How should the quality of life for seniors be improved? How will you plan to spend your senior citizens' life?

Language Focus

英语句子结构上具有后开放性特点，因此在使用英语表达时应该先将句子的主干提取出来，最后再添上句子的其他附加成分。

句子主干 指的是构成一个完整句子的框架，主要包括主语、谓语、宾语、表语等基本句子成分。

本语篇一共由6个句子构成，它们的句子主干分别是：

☆Citizens are eager.

☆Senior Citizens' University（SCU）was founded.

☆Students are free and the curriculum is extensive.

☆SCUs offer courses.

☆SCUs will be set up.

☆Citizens need things.

句子附加成分 指的是去除一个完整句子中的主干部分剩余的修饰、补充说明部分，主要包括定语、状语、宾语补足语、主语补足语、同位语、插入语这几个基本句子成分。

本语篇的句子附加成分如下：

★in China（介词短语作地点状语）

★with the increase（介词短语作原因状语）

★in ageing population（介词短语作后置定语）

★senior（形容词作定语）

★more（比较级作状语）

★the first（序数词作定语）

★in east China's Shandong Province（介词短语作地点状语）

★China's（名词所有格作定语）

★in 1983（介词短语作时间状语）

★at special universities（介词短语作地点状语）

★this kind of（名词短语作定语）

★from pressure and anxiety（介词短语作状语）

★academic（形容词作定语）

★employment（名词作定语）

★offering languages（现在分词短语作状语）

★foreign（形容词作定语）

★other（形容词作定语）

★many（形容词作定语）

★Chinese（形容词作定语）

★not only（副词作状语）

★ but...as well（副词作状语）

★ more（形容词作定语）

★ in Chinese calligraphy（介词短语作后置定语）

★ traditional（形容词作定语）

★ digital（形容词作定语）

★ to ensure citizens a life（不定式作目的状语）

★ fulfilling（形容词作定语）

★ besides education（介词短语作状语）

★ like elderly care and medical care（介词短语作定语）

★ elderly（形容词作定语）

★ medical（形容词作定语）

非谓语动词 是指动词形式有一定的变换，在句子中不作谓语，因此它不受主语的限制。非谓语动词在英语中很常见。它可以在句子中充当主语、宾语、表语、定语、状语、补语等句子成分。非谓语动词有以下三种形式：

◆ 动词不定式：to do/to be

◆ 动名词：doing/being

◆ 分词，一个是现在分词：doing/being；另一个是过去分词：done/been。

本语篇中非谓语动词的使用：

◇ **offering** foreign languages 现在分词作状语，表示的含义有主动、进行。

◇ **to ensure** senior citizens a fulfilling life 不定式作状语，表示的含义有动作的目的。

句子类型 主要包括简单句、复合句和并列句。在用英文表达时，尽量得体、恰当地交叉使用它们。简单句是指，一个主语或者两个以上主语加上一个谓语或者两个以上谓语构成的句子。复合句是指，一个主句加上一个或者多个从句构成的句子。并列句是指，两个以上简单句由并列连词连在一起构成的句子。

本语篇中句子类型的使用：

◎ In China, with the increase in ageing population, senior citizens are eager to learn more.

简单句：一个主语 senior citizens，一个谓语 are eager。

◎ The first Senior Citizens' University（SCU）was founded in east China's Shandong Province in 1983.

简单句：一个主语 The first Senior Citizens' University（SCU），一个谓语 was founded。

◎ Many Chinese SCUs offer not only courses in traditional Chinese calligraphy, painting, literature and science，but in snooker，digital graphic design and video editing as well.

简单句：一个主语SCUs，一个谓语offer。

◎At this kind of special universities，students are free from academic pressure and employment anxiety，and the curriculum is extensive，offering foreign languages，computer skills，music，dance，photography，painting and other crafts，sports and cooking.

并列句：由并列连词and将两个简单句连接在一起，简单句一 At this kind of special universities，students are free from academic pressure and employment anxiety；简单句二the curriculum is extensive，offering foreign languages，computer skills，music，dance，photography，painting and other crafts，sports and cooking。

并列句点拨：并列句是由并列连词把两个或两个以上独立的分句连接而成的。连词主要表现的逻辑关系有并列、选择、转折、递进和因果。常用的连词有and，not only...but also（并列关系），or，otherwise（选择关系），but（转折关系），so，for（因果关系）。

构词与常用搭配

senior（ *a.* ）年龄大一些的：由词根sen（老）加上形容词后缀 -ior构成。

常用搭配：senior students，senior players，senior managers，senior engineers

found（ *v.* ）创建：由词根fund=bottom（底部，基础）衍变而来。

常用搭配：be founded in，found a company，found a club，found a college

academic（ *a.* ）学术的：由词根academy（学院）加上形容词后缀-ic构成。

常用搭配：academic subjects，an academic institution，academic years

employment（ *n.* ）就业：由词根ploy=plic（折叠）加上前缀em-（向内）再加上名词后缀-ment构成。

常用搭配：be in employment，terms of employment，an employment agency

curriculum（ *n.* ）课程：由词根curr（流，跑）加上表示"小"的后缀-culum构成。

常用搭配：school curriculum，curriculum design，CV=curriculum vitae

extensive（ *v.* ）广阔的：由前缀ex-（出，向外）加上词根tens（延伸）再加上形容词后缀 -ive构成。

常用搭配：extensive damage，an extensive range of，extensive coverage

photography（ *n.* ）摄影：由词根photo（光）加上graph（写，画）再加上名词后缀 -y构成。

常用搭配：fashion photography，director of photography，digital photography

calligraphy（ *n.* ）书法：由词根graph（写，画）加上表示"漂亮的"前缀calli-，

再加上名词后缀-y构成。

常用搭配：painting and calligraphy，calligraphy competition

graphic（*a.*）绘画的，书画的：由词根graph（写，画）加上形容词后缀-ic构成。

常用搭配：graphic design，graphic arts，a graphic account/description

fulfilling（*a.*）令人愉快满足的：由形容词full（充满的）加上动词 fill（充满）构成合成词fulfill，再加上形容词后缀-ing构成。

常用搭配：fulfilling experience，fulfilling relationship，fulfilling and rewarding

Crossword Puzzle

Across

3. the fact of someone being paid to work for a company or an organization

4. making you feel happy and satisfied

5. related to drawing or printing

6. relating to schools, colleges, and universities, or connected with studying and thinking, not with practical skills

9. the activity or job of taking photographs or filming

10. to bring something into existence

Down

1. beautiful writing, often created with a special pen or brush

2. high or higher in rank

7. covering a large area; having a great range

8. the subjects studied in a school, college, etc. and what each subject includes

The Afforestation Pioneers on Saihanba Highland 塞罕坝的造林先锋

There were three generations of afforestation pioneers who had been willing to dedicate themselves without asking for repay on Saihanba Highland which used to be a place where birds had no trees to perch on, and yellow sand covered the sky, while it has become the largest artificial forest in the world today. Enduring indescribable adversity, those afforestation pioneers have turned Saihanba into a green screen for the Capital city, which is a miracle of ecological civilization in China.

Reading Comprehension

Background Information

20世纪60年代的塞罕坝自然环境十分恶劣：没有食物、房屋急缺，冬天大雪封山处于半封闭、半隔绝的状态；从各地赶来的建设者们除了简单的行李衣物外，其他一无所有。然而，通过塞罕坝三代造林先锋们的艰苦努力，在140万亩的总经营面积上，成功营造了112万亩人工林，创造了让沙漠变成绿洲的绿色奇迹。森林覆盖率达到80%，林木总蓄积量达到1012万立方米。作为中国面积最大的集中连片人造林，塞罕坝上的人工林海是塞罕坝造林先锋们在塞北荒原上谱写的不朽于人类历史的绿色篇章。

Critical Thinking

Question One：What are the personality traits of pioneers？Do you respect them？Why or why not？

Question Two：How much do you know about ecological civilization？Are you willing to make a contribution to it？

Question Three：How will the construction of ecological civilization promote our strength to globally build a community with a shared future for mankind？

Language Focus

英语句子结构上具有后开放性特点，因此在使用英语表达时应该先将句子的主干提取出来，最后再添上句子的其他附加成分。

句子主干 指的是构成一个完整句子的框架，主要包括几个基本句子成分：主语、谓语、宾语、表语。

本语篇一共由2个句子构成，它们的句子主干分别是：

☆There were generations.

☆Pioneers have turned Saihanba.

句子附加成分 指的是去除一个完整句子中的主干部分剩余的修饰、补充说明部分，主要包括几个基本句子成分：定语、状语、宾语补足语、主语补足语、同位语、插入语。

本语篇的句子附加成分如下：

★three（数词作定语）

★of afforestation pioneers（介词短语作后置定语）

★who had been willing to dedicate themselves without asking for repay on Saihanba Highland（限定性定语从句）

★which used to be a place（限定性定语从句）

★where birds had no trees to perch on，and yellow sand covered the sky（限定性定语从句）

★while it has become the largest artificial forest in the world today（由while并列连词引导的并列分句）

★enduring indescribable adversity（现在分词短语作伴随状语）

★those（指示代词作定语）

★afforestation（名词作定语）

★into a green screen（介词短语作宾语补足语）

★for the Capital city（介词短语作后置定语）

★which is a miracle of ecological civilization in China（非限定性定语从句）

非谓语动词 是指动词在句子中不作谓语时的形式，因此它不受主语的限制。非谓语动词在英语句子中使用频繁且广泛。它可以在句子中充当除了谓语之外的其他成分，主语、宾语、表语、定语、状语、补语等。非谓语动词分为3大类：

◆动词不定式：to do/to be

◆动名词：doing/being

◆分词，一个是现在分词：doing/being；另一个是过去分词：done/been。

本语篇中非谓语动词的使用：

◇without **asking** for repay动名词作宾语。

◇**to perch** on 动词不定式短语作后置定语表用途。

◇**enduring** indescribable adversity现在分词短语作状语表进行、伴随。

句子类型 主要包括：简单句、复合句和并列句。在用英文表达时，尽量得体、恰当地交叉使用它们。简单句是指，一个主语或者两个、多个并列主语加上一个谓语或者两个、多个并列谓语构成的句子。复合句是指，一个主句加上一个或者多个从句构成的句子。并列句是指，由并列连词把两个或多个简单句连在一起构成的句子。

本语篇中句子类型的使用：

◎There were three generations of afforestation pioneers who had been willing to dedicate themselves without asking for repay on Saihanba Highland which used to be a place where birds had no trees to perch on, and yellow sand covered the sky, while it has become the largest artificial forest in the world today.

复合句：一个主句There were three generations of afforestation pioneers。三个从句，从句一是who had been willing to dedicate themselves without asking for repay on Saihanba Highlan；从句二是which used to be a place；从句三是where birds had no trees to perch on, and yellow sand covered the sky。

同时从句三中还有两个并列分句，并列分句一是由and连接的birds had no trees to perch on 和yellow sand covered the sky的并列；并列分句二是由while连接的it has become the largest artificial forest in the world today和used to be a place where birds had no trees to perch on, and yellow sand covered the sky的对比。

◎Enduring indescribable adversity, those afforestation pioneers have turned Saihanba into a green screen for the Capital city, which is a miracle of ecological civilization in China.

复合句：一个主句Those afforestation pioneers have turned Saihanba into a green screen for the Capital city.

一个从句which is a miracle of ecological civilization in China

错综复合句点拨：这种复合句既包含并列关系的句子，又包含主从关系的复合句。它的结构虽然错综复杂，但是只要准确找出句子主干，厘清句子之间的逻辑关系就能明确错综复合句的构成和表达的语意。

构词与常用搭配

generation（*n.*）代，一代（人）：由动词generate（生育）加上名词后缀-ion构成。动词generate源自词根gen（生育），词源同gene（基因，遗传）。

常用搭配：present generation，new generation，future generation，past generation

afforestation（*n.*）人工造林：由动词afforest（绿化）加上名词后缀-ation构成；afforest是由forest（使长满树林）加上表示"去，往"的前缀af-构成。afforest的反义词deforest（砍伐森林，毁林）由词根forest（森林）加上表示"去除，夺走，损毁"的前缀de-构成。

常用搭配：afforestation rate，massive afforestation，afforestation workers

pioneer（*n.*）先锋：源自一个表示"步兵"的法语词，该种步兵的职责是负责为后面的大部队铺路，由此衍生出"带头人，拓荒者，先驱"等含义。

常用搭配：the Young Pioneer，an explorer and pioneer

dedication（*n.*）奉献：由词根dic（说，讲）加上表示强调的前缀de-，再加上名词后缀-ation构成；同一词根的类似构词还有indication（暗示）：由词根dic（说，讲）加上表示"向内"的前缀in-，再加上名词后缀-ation构成。

常用搭配：selfless dedication，dedication to，professional dedication

perch（*v.*）栖息；停留：源自一个表示"棍、杆"的拉丁语词，后来专门指鸟停留的横杆，又进一步引申为"栖息"。

常用搭配：perch on，on the perch（*n.*），perch（*n.*）of sleep

artificial（*a.*）人工制的，人造的：源自词根art（技巧）加上词缀-fic=-fac（制作），再加上形容词后缀-ial构成。

常用搭配：AI=artificial intelligence，natural or artificial，artificial limb，artificial forest

endure（*v.*）忍耐：由词根dur（硬，坚持），加上前缀en-=in-（进入）构成。与duration（持久），durable（耐久的），during（由dur"坚持"+-ing"进行，状态"引申为"在……期间"）都源自同一个词根。

常用搭配：endure hardship，endure adversity，endure pain

indescribable（*a.*）难以描述，无法形容的：由词根scribe（写），加上前缀de-（向下），加上形容词后缀-able，再加上表示否定含义的前缀in-构成。

常用搭配：indescribable beauty，indescribable sensation，indescribable happiness

adversity（*n.*）困境；灾难：由词根vers=turn（转）加上前缀ad-（朝着，向着），再加上名词后缀-sity构成。同一个词根变化而来的还有：converse（相反的），reverse（背面的），inverse（反向的）。

常用搭配：in adversity，over adversity，in the face of adversity，face with adversity，in time of adversity，struggle with adversity，pain and adversity

miracle（*n.*）奇迹：由词根mir=wonder，look（惊奇，看）加上表示"东西，状态"的名词后缀-acle构成。同一个词根变化而来的还有：mirror（镜子；反映），marvel（令人惊奇的事物）。

常用搭配：economic miracle，work miracle，scientific miracle，a miracle of

ecological（*a.*）生态学的：由词根log=logue（说；话）加上前缀eco-（生态的），再加上形容词后缀-ical构成。

常用搭配：ecological disasters，ecological balance，ecological culture，ecological economy，ecological protection，ecological environment

civilization（*n.*）文明社会：由词根civil（公民的；有礼貌的）加上名词后缀-zation构成。人类自从修建城市，开始城市生活后就进入了civilization（文明社会），在此之前的农业社会从事culture（耕种、培育）。

常用搭配：modern civilization，ancient civilization，Chinese civilization，world civilization，Western civilization，alien civilization，early civilization

Crossword Puzzle

Across

2. concerned about the ecology of a place

6. the large amount of time and effort that someone spends on something

8. a place for a bird to land or rest on

9. the conversion of bare or cultivated land into forest

10. to experience and deal with something that is painful or unpleasant, especially without complaining

11. a difficult or unpleasant situation

Down

1. a state of human society that is very developed and organized

3. any amazing or wonderful occurrence

4. so extreme or unusual it is almost impossible to describe

5. group of people in society who are born and live around the same time; a particular group existing at a particular time

7. one of the first people to do something important that is later continued and developed by other people

9. created by people; not happening naturally

Section B　Module Project：Global Issues Discussion

作为懂外语的中国人，在国家提出"讲好中国故事，传播好中国声音，展示真实、立体、全面的中国"呼吁下，你是否准备好了向世界积极传播中国力量、中国方案和中国智慧，为构成国际传播矩阵贡献自己的一分力量？

Short Video Project：What facts about Chinese people will you tell the whole world? Could you make them short videos and then post these videos on websites to communicate globally?

Section C　Learners' Presentation

在创作英文微视频时，英语词汇的选用要尽量贴近生活口语化，表达句式也不宜太过复杂，但是常用的从句、并列句、非谓语动词还是应该多多使用。在构词成句的过程中运用本书提出的先写"句子主干"，再"附加成分"的方法会让你的英文表达符合英语语言逻辑，而且流畅自如。目前国内流行两个微视频制作主流软件，两款软件的学习使用都简单易懂。这样，你也可以轻松制作英文微视频，为传播中国好声音贡献力量。

Section D   Reflective Assessment

成长档案袋

	Y	N	Achievements
Am I satisfied with my project products?			
Shall I further improve my project products?			
Are my project products popular online?			
Can I globally tell some facts about Chinese people with confidence?			
Have I mastered the vocabulary, sentence patterns and some background information on Chinese people's facts?			

Module Two

What Do You Know about Chinese Culture?

你了解多少中国文化?

　　《好大一棵树》大树巍然屹立于画面的中间位置，洋溢着一种极其静谧的昂扬姿态，并在年复一年中脱胎换骨，检索一种人文积淀和无意识的控制。那种站直了，别趴下的人格和道德的力量，正是艺术家挖掘和弘扬中国传统文化主体根脉的贡献所在。（艺术评论家王健）

　　In the middle of the painting majestically stands the tree，exuding exuberance with tranquil posture. Year after year，it is reborn retrieving accumulations in humanistic perspective and unconscious control over humanity. The strength of personality and morality that stands up straight and does not lie down is precisely what the painter's contribution to excavating and carrying forward the roots of traditional Chinese culture. (Art critic：WANG Jian)

Section A   Interpretive Input

The Tiger in Chinese Culture 中国"虎"文化

2022 is the year of the tiger in the Chinese lunar calendar. The tiger represents courage and strength, because Chinese people often use the vivid dragon and the energetic tiger to describe the lively, vigorous and energetic. Today, in the face of painful hardships, we should have an awe-inspiring momentum and bravely overcome all kinds of obstacles on our way forward like tigers. Only in this way can we unite and realize our dreams.

Reading Comprehension

Background Information

虎乃百兽之王，中国的"虎文化"历史悠久。老虎威猛凶悍，让人类既畏惧又崇拜。早期，在军事上，人们用虎符来调兵遣将；在民间，老虎的形象被用来辟邪和守护，很多小孩子是伴着布老虎、虎头帽和老虎鞋长大的。无论是在诗词歌赋里，还是在戏曲绘画中，虎大多是力量、勇敢、无畏的象征，它在我国艺术发展和文化传承上都有着重要的地位。

Critical Thinking

Question One: The tiger is at the top of the animal food chain. It is a landmark species to protect and measure the health of the ecosystem. From a "biological" point of view, the number of tiger species can reflect whether the ecosystem is balanced. The existence of the tiger represents an evolved and mature ecological society, which has been nurtured by nature for millions of years. What should we do to protect tigers?

Question Two: For thousands of years, the Chinese people have worshipped the tiger, extended the image of the tiger to folk culture, daily necessities, art and other fields, and formed a very distinctive tiger culture. What can we do to revitalize the image of the tiger?

Language Focus

英语句子结构上具有后开放性特点，因此在使用英语表达时应该先将句子的主干提取出来，最后再添上句子的其他附加成分。

句子主干 指的是构成一个完整句子的框架，主要包括几个基本句子成分：主

语、谓语、宾语、表语。

本语篇一共由4个句子构成，它们的句子主干分别是：

☆2022 is the year.

☆The tiger represents courage and strength.

☆We should have momentum and overcome obstacles.

☆We can unite and realize dreams.

句子附加成分 指的是去除一个完整句子中的主干部分剩余的修饰、补充说明部分，主要包括几个基本句子成分：定语、状语、宾语补足语、主语补足语、同位语、插入语。

本语篇的句子附加成分如下：

★of the tiger（介词短语作后置定语）

★in the Chinese lunar calendar（介词短语作后置定语）

★because Chinese people often use the vivid dragon and the energetic tiger...（状语从句中由and连接两个并列宾语）

★often（频度副词作状语）

★vivid（形容词作定语）

★energetic（形容词作定语）

★today（时间状语）

★in the face of（介词短语作状语）

★painful（形容词作定语）

★hardships（名词作定语）

★awe-inspiring（形容词作定语）

★bravely（副词作状语）

★all kinds of（作定语）

★on our way forward（介词短语作状语）

★like tigers（介词短语作方式状语）

★Only in this way can we unite...（Only放句首，句子用倒装语序，情态动词 can 放在主语 we 的前面）

★our（物主代词作定语）

非谓语动词 是指动词在句子中不作谓语时的形式，因此它不受主语的限制。非谓语动词在英语句子中使用频繁且广泛。它可以在句子中充当除了谓语之外的其他成分，主语、宾语、表语、定语、状语、补语等。非谓语动词分为3大类：

◆ 动词不定式：to do / to be

◆ 动名词：doing / being

◆ 分词，一个是现在分词：doing / being；另一个是过去分词：done / been。

本语篇中非谓语动词的使用：

◇ **to describe** the lively，vigorous and energetic 动词不定式短语作状语表示目的。

句子类型 主要包括：简单句、复合句和并列句。在用英文表达时，尽量得体、恰当地交叉使用它们。简单句是指，一个主语或者两个、多个并列主语加上一个谓语或者两个、多个并列谓语构成的句子。复合句是指，一个主句加上一个或者多个从句构成的句子。并列句是指，由并列连词把两个或多个简单句连在一起构成的句子。

本语篇中句子类型的使用：

◎ 2022 is the year of the tiger in the Chinese lunar calendar.

简单句：一个主语2022，一个谓语由系表结构组成is the year。

◎ The tiger represents courage and strength because Chinese people often use the vivid dragon and the energetic tiger to describe the lively，vigorous and energetic.

复合句：一个主句The tiger represents courage and strength，一个从句because Chinese people often use the vivid dragon and the energetic tiger to describe the lively，vigorous and energetic。

◎ Today，in the face of painful hardships，we should have an awe-inspiring momentum and bravely overcome all kinds of obstacles on our way forward like tigers.

简单句：一个主语we，一个并列谓语由情态动词should和两个实义动词have和overcome构成。

◎ Only in this way can we unite and realize our dreams.

简单句：一个主语we，一个并列谓语由情态动词can和两个实义动词unite和realize构成；"only +状语"位于句首，其后紧跟的句子部分倒装。

主从复合句点拨：状语从句就是该从句在整个复合句中起副词作用，作状语成分。根据状语从句在复合句中所起到的作用，可分为让步、比较、方式、原因、目的、结果、条件、地点和时间等从句。状语从句在英文表达中使用频率很高。

构词与常用搭配

lunar（*a.*）月亮的，阴历的：来自拉丁文luna（月亮），词源同lumen，light。由表示"月亮"的词根lun加上形容词词尾-ar组成。

常用搭配：lunar new year，lunar orbit，lunar calendar，lunar eclipse

calendar（*n.*）日历，历法：源自拉丁语 calendae（罗马月份的第一天）。由表示"每月第一天"的词根calend加上表物的后缀-ar组成。

常用搭配：make a calendar，sporting calendar，political calendar，personal calendar

energetic（*a.*）精力充沛的，充满活力的：源自希腊语。前缀en-表示"使……进入状态"，词根erg意为"工作、行动"，而-etic是形容词词尾。

常用搭配：energetic man，energetic supporter，energetic discussion

vigorous（*a.*）精力旺盛的；强健的：源自拉丁语。词根vig表示"活力"，-or表"状况"，-ous为形容词词尾。

常用搭配：vigorous life，vigorous politician

hardship（*n.*）艰难；困苦：由表示"艰难的"词根hard加上表示"某种关系、状态"的名词后缀-ship组成。

常用搭配：financial hardship，economic hardship，severe hardship

awe-inspiring（*a.*）令人惊叹的；使人敬佩的：awe表示"敬畏"，inspiring表示"有启发的，鼓舞的"。

常用搭配：awe-inspiring manners，awe-inspiring event

momentum（*n.*）动力，势头：前缀mo-，来源于表示"移动"的move；而momentum源于拉丁语 momentum，表示"运动"，词源同moment。

常用搭配：gained momentum，with great momentum

obstacle（*n.*）障碍（物）：源自古法语，词源同stand，指"对着站的，站在对面的"，后引申为"障碍"。前缀ob-意为"相对，对着的"；-st=to stand，指"站，站立"；后缀-acle为名词词尾，表物。

常用搭配：overcome/defeat obstacles，throw obstacles in sb's way

unite（*v.*）团结；（为某事）联合；联手；（与某人或集体）联结：来自拉丁语unitus。un-=uni-代表"一，统一"，而后缀-ite为动词词尾，表示"做……，使……。

常用搭配：unite with，unite party

Crossword Puzzle

<table>
<tr><td>

Across

3. to join together with other people in order to do something as a group

5. a system by which time is divided into fixed periods, showing the beginning and end of a year

8. impressive, making you feel respect and admiration

9. of, involving, caused by, or affecting the moon

</td><td>

Down

1. anything that makes it difficult for you to do something

2. very active, determined or full of energy

4. operating with or marked by vigor or effect

6. the ability to keep increasing or developing

7. a situation that is difficult and unpleasant because you do not have enough money, food, clothes, etc.

</td></tr>
</table>

Couplets in Chinese Culture 中国对联文化

Chinese people usually stick Spring Festival couplets on doors before the Spring Festival. It represents people's wishes for the new year. It is said that this custom can be traced back to the Western Han Dynasty. It fully shows that the Chinese people have always attached great significance to cultural inheritance. I put the couplets written by myself on the door. This Spring Festival was really the happiest and most unforgettable festival I have ever spent in China.

Reading Comprehension

Background Information

中国人过春节的传统习俗之一就是贴春联，这表达了广大人民辞旧迎新、迎祥纳福之意，也为节日增添了喜庆气氛。说起贴春联，那真是历史悠久：2000多年前，古人就把桃木片挂在门两边，用以辟邪护宅。桃木片上可以写春词，也就是祝福语，祈求平安顺利，健康幸福，这就是春联的雏形。唐朝后桃符被门神代替，而对联保留了下来。明朝开始，人们把对联写在大红纸上。对联讲究对仗工整，平仄押韵。上联以仄声字结尾，下联以平声字结尾。

Critical Thinking

Question One: In recent years, the sales of "interesting Spring Festival couplets" have also been particularly prosperous. "Interesting Spring Festival couplets" use more Internet language and talk show language. Why do you think this kind of "interesting Spring Festival couplets" is loved by young people? Will it totally replace the traditional Spring Festival couplets?

Question Two: There are many rules for posting Spring couplets. Do you know them? For example, what is the proper time to post Spring Festival couplets? Which side should be the top and bottom couplets attached to?

Question Three: How much do you know about the Chinese calligraphy brush? Can you write brilliantly with brush? Which are better, handwritten couplets or printed ones? Why?

Language Focus

英语句子结构上具有后开放性特点，因此在使用英语表达时应该先将句子的主干提取出来,最后再添上句子的其他附加成分。

句子主干 指的是构成一个完整句子的框架,主要包括几个基本句子成分:主语、谓语、宾语、表语。

本语篇一共由6个句子构成,它们的句子主干分别是:

☆People stick Spring Festival couplets.

☆It represents wishes.

☆It is said.

☆It shows.

☆I put the couplets.

☆This Spring Festival was the happiest and most unforgettable festival.

句子附加成分 指的是去除一个完整句子中的主干部分剩余的修饰、补充说明部分,主要包括几个基本句子成分:定语、状语、宾语补足语、主语补足语、同位语、插入语。

本语篇的句子附加成分如下:

★Chinese(形容词作定语)

★usually(频度副词作状语)

★on doors(介词短语作地点状语)

★before the Spring Festival(介词短语作时间状语)

★for the new year(介词短语作定语)

★this custom can be traced back to the Western Han Dynasty(主语从句)

★the Chinese people have always attached great significance to cultural inheritance(宾语从句)

★written by myself(过去分词短语作定语)

★on the door(介词短语作地点状语)

★really(状语,用来加强语气)

★the happiest and most unforgettable(and连接两个形容词最高级作定语)

★I have ever spent in China(定语从句)

★in China(介词短语作地点状语)

非谓语动词 是指动词在句子中不作谓语时的形式,因此它不受主语的限制。非谓语动词在英语句子中使用频繁且广泛。它可以在句子中充当除了谓语之外的其他成分，主语、宾语、表语、定语、状语、补语等。非谓语动词分为3大类：

◆动词不定式：to do / to be

◆动名词：doing / being

◆分词，一个是现在分词：doing / being；另一个是过去分词：done / been。

本语篇中非谓语动词的使用：

◇the couplets **written** by myself 过去分词作定语表示的含义有被动、完成。

句子类型 主要包括：简单句、复合句和并列句。在用英文表达时，尽量得体、恰当地交叉使用它们。简单句是指，一个主语或者两个、多个并列主语加上一个谓语或者两个、多个并列谓语构成的句子。复合句是指，一个主句加上一个或者多个从句构成的句子。并列句是指，由并列连词把两个或多个简单句连在一起构成的句子。

本语篇中句子类型的使用：

◎Chinese people usually stick Spring Festival couplets on doors before the Spring Festival.

简单句：一个主语people，一个谓语stick。

◎It represents people's wishes for the new year.

简单句：一个主语it，一个谓语represents。

◎It is said that this custom can be traced back to the Western Han Dynasty.

复合句：一个主句It is said，一个从句that this custom can be traced back to the Western Han Dynasty。

◎It fully shows that the Chinese people have always attached great significance to cultural inheritance.

复合句：一个主句It fully shows，一个从句that the Chinese people have always attached great significance to cultural inheritance。

◎I put the couplets written by myself on the door.

简单句：一个主语I，一个谓语put。

◎This Spring Festival was really the happiest and most unforgettable festival I have ever spent in China.

复合句：一个主句This Spring Festival was really the happiest and most unforgettable festival，一个从句I have ever spent in China。

主从复合句点拨：主语从句就是该从句在整个复合句中作主语成分。为避免句子头重脚轻，形式主语it经常被用来作形式主语，出现在句首，代替真正的主语从句。

构词与常用搭配

represent（*n.*）代表；表示：来源于拉丁语动词 praesentare（呈现，展示）。由表示"赠送，呈现"的present，加上表示"再"的前缀re-组成。

常用搭配：represent one's sides，represent many countries

trace（*v.*）追踪，追溯：来自古法语 tracier（寻找，追踪），词源同 draw，tract。词根为trac，意为"拖"。

常用搭配：trace sb/sth（to sth），trace sth（back）（to sth）

dynasty（*n.*）王朝；朝代：来自希腊语dynamis（力量，权力，统治者）。由dyn-（力），-ast（名词词尾，人），-y（名词词尾）三部分组成。

常用搭配：build/establish/found a dynasty

attach（*v.*）依附，联系：来自古法语atachier，（法律术语：系紧；逮捕）。词根attach=at=ad，意为"去"，后缀-tach指"固定"。

常用搭配：attach sth to sth，attach importance，significance，value，weight，etc.（to sth）

significance（*n.*）意义；重大，重要性：源于古法语。可分三部分来记：词根sign（标记）+fic-（做，作）+表示名词词尾的后缀-ance。

常用搭配：strategic/cultural/global significance

inheritance（*n.*）继承；继承物（如金钱、财产等）；遗产：源自公元前14世纪晚期古法语enheriter，原义为"使继承"，后引申为"遗传"。由拉丁词根herit（表示"继承人"）加上名词后缀-ance（表示"状态、事实"）组成。

常用搭配：receive inheritance，claim inheritance

unforgettable（*a.*）难以忘怀的；令人难忘的：前缀un-表示否定，forget意为"忘记"，形容词后缀-able表示"有能力"。

常用搭配：unforgettable experience，unforgettable memories

Crossword Puzzle

Across

4. to find the origin or cause of something

5. the money, property, etc. that you receive from somebody when they die; the fact of receiving something when somebody dies

6. a series of rulers of a country who all belong to the same family

7. the importance of something, especially when this has an effect on what happens in the future

Down

1. to be a member of a group of people and act or speak on their behalf at an event, a meeting, etc.

2. impossible to forget

3. to fasten or join one thing to another

Tea Culture 茶文化

China National Tea Museum, the only museum in China with the theme of tea culture, was established in Longjing Village in 1991. All aspects of tea can be learned about here. The museum consists of six halls: Tea History, Kaleidoscope, Tea Properties, Tea Friendship, Tea Sets and Tea Customs. It is not only the exhibition and exchange center of tea culture between China and the world, but also the theme tourism complex of tea culture. The museum will hold seminars for young people in order to popularize tea culture and present the influence of tea on Chinese culture.

Reading Comprehension

Background Information

据考证，世界上最早利用和发现茶的国家是中国，因此，中国被称为世界茶文化的起点。而所谓的茶文化就是指在饮茶的过程中形成的一些文化特征。中国人的饮茶习俗通过古代"丝绸之路"和其他贸易渠道的文化交流传播到欧洲和许多其他地区。中国茶之道蕴含着东方哲学的智慧，也体现了道家、儒家和佛教的中心思想，是哲学和生活方式的结合。

Critical Thinking

Question One: Tea culture is an integral part of the excellent traditional culture of the Chinese nation, which reflects the Chinese people's longing for a better life and their pursuit of health. Tea is not only refreshing, but also beneficial to physical and mental health and interpersonal communication. Please explain the ecological concept contained in tea.

Question Two: Today, what kind of spirit should be advocated to carry forward Chinese traditional tea culture?

Question Three: With the development of modern society, coffee and tea are no longer Chinese or western regional drinks, what does the mutual integration of tea culture and coffee culture mean?

Language Focus

英语句子结构上具有后开放性特点，因此在使用英语表达时应该先将句子的主干提取出来，最后再添上句子的其他附加成分。

句子主干 指的是构成一个完整句子的框架，主要包括几个基本句子成分：主

语、谓语、宾语、表语。

本语篇一共由5个句子构成，它们的句子主干分别是：

☆ China National Tea Museum was established.

☆ Aspects can be learned about.

☆ The museum consists of halls.

☆ It is not only the center, but also the complex.

☆ The museum will hold seminars.

句子附加成分 指的是去除一个完整句子中的主干部分剩余的修饰、补充说明部分，主要包括几个基本句子成分：定语、状语、宾语补足语、主语补足语、同位语、插入语。

本语篇的句子附加成分如下：

★ the only museum in China with the theme of tea culture（插入语）

★ in Longjing Village（介词短语作地点状语）

★ in 1991（介词短语作时间状语）

★ all（限定词作定语）

★ of tea（介词短语作后置定语）

★ here（副词作地点状语）

★ six（数词作定语）

★ Tea History, Kaleidoscope, Tea Properties, Tea Friendship, Tea Sets and Tea Customs（名词短语作同位语）

★ the exhibition and exchange（名词短语作定语）

★ of tea culture（介词短语作后置定语）

★ between China and the world（介词短语作后置定语）

★ theme tourism（作定语）

★ of tea culture（介词短语作后置定语）

★ for young people（介词短语作宾语）

★ of tea on Chinese culture（介词短语作后置定语）

非谓语动词 是指动词在句子中不作谓语时的形式，因此它不受主语的限制。非谓语动词在英语句子中使用频繁且广泛。它可以在句子中充当除了谓语之外的其他

成分，主语、宾语、表语、定语、状语、补语等。非谓语动词分为3大类：

◆动词不定式：to do/to be

◆动名词：doing/being

◆分词，一个是现在分词：doing/being；另一个是过去分词：done/been。

本语篇中非谓语动词的使用：

◇in order **to popularize** tea culture and **present** the influence 动词不定式短语表示目的，作状语。

句子类型 主要包括：简单句、复合句和并列句。在用英文表达时，尽量得体、恰当地交叉使用它们。简单句是指，一个主语或者两个、多个并列主语加上一个谓语或者两个、多个并列谓语构成的句子。复合句是指，一个主句加上一个或者多个从句构成的句子。并列句是指，由并列连词把两个或多个简单句连在一起构成的句子。

本语篇中句子类型的使用：

◎China National Tea Museum, the only museum in China with the theme of tea culture, was established in Longjing Village in 1991.

简单句：一个主语China National Tea Museum，一个谓语was established。

◎All aspects of tea can be learned about here.

简单句：一个主语aspects，一个谓语can be learned about。

◎The museum consists of six halls: Tea History, Kaleidoscope, Tea Properties, Tea Friendship, Tea Sets and Tea Customs.

简单句：一个主语museum，一个谓语consists of。

◎It is not only the exhibition and exchange center of tea culture between China and the world, but also the theme tourism complex of tea culture.

简单句：一个主语it，一个并列谓语由系表结构组成is not only the center...but also the theme tourism complex...

◎The museum will hold seminars for young people in order to popularize tea culture and present the influence of tea on Chinese culture.

简单句：一个主语museum，一个谓语will hold。

简单句点拨：简单句的表达清晰简洁，是复杂句子的基本组成单位。简单句的句子主干和核心是句子的主语和谓语。

构词与常用搭配

aspect（*n.*）方面：该词原为天文学术语，指"星体的相对位置"。由表示"来，临近"的前缀a-加上表示"看"的词根spect组成。

常用搭配：on the aspect of = in the aspect of，key aspect

kaleidoscope（*n.*）千变万化：原义为"万花筒"，由其发明者David Brewster（19世纪苏格兰科学家）根据希腊语合成的一个词。由希腊语kal（漂亮的），加上 -eido（形状），再加上后缀-scope（观测仪器）组成。

常用搭配：a kaleidoscope of color

property（*n.*）特性，性质：由三部分组成：prop-（表示"自己的；拥有"）+-er（名词词尾）+-ty（名词词尾，表示"状态"）。

常用搭配：physical property，property right，real property，intellectual property right

exhibition（*n.*）展览，陈列：源于古法语exhibicion。前缀ex-，表示"出"，词根hibit表示"持，握"，-ion是名词词尾。

常用搭配：have/hold/give/put on an exhibition，on exhibition

exchange（*n.*）交换：来自古法语易货商"交换，易货"。词根change，意为"改变"，前缀ex-，表示"向外"。

常用搭配：exchange A for B，exchange gifts，exchange ideas

tourism（*n.*）旅游（业）：由词根tour（迂回，转）加上名词词尾-ism（行为，现象）组成。

常用搭配：tourism industry，develop tourism，promote tourism

complex（*a.*）复杂的：词源 apply，implicate，即"多成分的，复杂的"。com-表示"强调"，-plect意为"编织，组成"。

常用搭配：complex idea，complex machines，complex sentence

seminar（*n.*）研讨会：来自德语，源于拉丁文Seminarium，由词根semen（种子）和后缀-arium（……的地方）构成。

常用搭配：international seminar，Seminar Leader，Executive seminar

popularize（*v.*）使大众化；推广：popul-指"人民"，-ar为形容词词尾，-ize则是动词词尾，表示"……化"。

常用搭配：popularize the concept / idea

influence（*n.*）影响，支配：词源同 fluid，fluent. 意为"流进"，引申为"影响"。由三部分组成：in-（进入，使）+-flu（流动）+-ence（名词词尾，表"行为"）。

常用搭配：have influence over，have influence upon / on

Crossword Puzzle

Across

4. a particular part or feature of a situation, an idea, a problem, etc, a way in which it may be considered

5. an act of giving something to somebody or doing something for somebody and receiving something in return

6. a situation, pattern, etc. containing a lot of different parts that are always changing

10. a quality or characteristic that something has

Down

1. the act of showing something, for example works of art, to the public

2. the effect that somebody/something has on the way a person thinks or behaves or on the way that something works or develops

3. a meeting for discussion or training

7. to make a lot of people know about something and enjoy it

8. the business activity connected with providing accommodation, services and entertainment for people who are visiting a place

9. made of many different things or parts that are connected; difficult to understand

Embroidery Culture 刺绣文化

Embroidery is very time-consuming. It may take a whole day to complete the length of 10 cm. By the 1970s, the number of embroiderers in Sichuan had reached 5000. Shu embroidery is a specialty of Chengdu, Sichuan Province. Shu embroidery is one of the longest handed-down embroideries in China. It spread to other countries through the Southern Silk Road. It is even a fashion product of ancient Rome. For thousands of years, Shu embroidery has represented Sichuan culture, so we should save it.

Reading Comprehension

Background Information

蜀绣,是中国四大名绣之一,从三国时期就已经名满天下了,它曾作为"蜀中瑰宝"被蜀国用于交换战略物资。后来,历代皇帝也会把蜀绣当作珍宝赏赐给功臣。蜀绣的工艺和产量在宋朝都达到了鼎盛时期。民国初年,蜀绣在国际巴拿马赛中获得金奖,闻名中外。之后,蜀绣开始走进寻常百姓家,因其色彩明丽和针法精湛而广受人们的喜爱。如今,蜀绣被列入国家级非物质文化遗产代表性项目名录。

Critical Thinking

Question One: Entering the new century, with the rapid development of science and technology, computer embroidery flooded the market, which is both economical and beautiful. Are young people willing to learn the traditional craft of embroidery? Why or why not?

Question Two: What is the significance of saving the traditional art of embroidery? What will you do to help communicate Chinese embroidery globally?

Question Three: The current situation of Shu embroidery is not optimistic, its historical and cultural transmission channels are relatively few, and there is a shortage of talent engaged in this industry. Please make suggestions for the protection of Shu embroidery culture.

Language Focus

英语句子结构上具有后开放性特点,因此在使用英语表达时应该先将句子的主干提取出来,最后再添上句子的其他附加成分。

句子主干 指的是构成一个完整句子的框架,主要包括几个基本句子成分:主语、谓语、宾语、表语。

本语篇一共由8个句子构成，它们的句子主干分别是：

☆ Embroidery is time-consuming.

☆ It may take a day.

☆ The number had reached 5000.

☆ Shu embroidery is a specialty.

☆ Shu embroidery is one.

☆ It spread.

☆ It is a product.

☆ Shu embroidery has represented culture.

句子附加成分 指的是去除一个完整句子中的主干部分剩余的修饰、补充说明部分，主要包括几个基本句子成分：定语、状语、宾语补足语、主语补足语、同位语、插入语。

本语篇的句子附加成分如下：

★ very（副词作状语）

★ whole（形容词作定语）

★ of 10 cm（介词短语作定语）

★ by the 1970s（介词短语作时间状语）

★ of embroiderers（介词短语作后置定语）

★ in Sichuan（介词短语作后置定语）

★ of Chengdu（介词短语作后置定语）

★ Sichuan Province（作定语）

★ of the longest embroideries（介词短语作后置定语）

★ in China（介词短语作状语）

★ to other countries（介词短语作地点状语）

★ through the Southern Silk Road（介词短语作方式状语）

★ even（副词作状语）

★ fashion（名词作定语）

★ of ancient Rome（介词短语作后置定语）

★ for thousands of years（介词短语作时间状语）

★so we should save it（状语从句表示结果）

非谓语动词 是指动词在句子中不作谓语时的形式，因此它不受主语的限制。非谓语动词在英语句子中使用频繁且广泛。它可以在句子中充当除了谓语之外的其他成分，主语、宾语、表语、定语、状语、补语等。非谓语动词分为3大类：

◆动词不定式：to do / to be

◆动名词：doing / being

◆分词，一个是现在分词：doing / being；另一个是过去分词：done / been。

本语篇中非谓语动词的使用：

◇**to complete** the length动词不定式短语作真正的主语。

◇**handed-down** embroideries 过去分词短语作定语表示的含义有被动、完成。

句子类型 主要包括：简单句、复合句和并列句。在用英文表达时，尽量得体、恰当地交叉使用它们。简单句是指，一个主语或者两个、多个并列主语加上一个谓语或者两个、多个并列谓语构成的句子。复合句是指，一个主句加上一个或者多个从句构成的句子。并列句是指，由并列连词把两个或多个简单句连在一起构成的句子。

本语篇中句子类型的使用：

◎Embroidery is very time-consuming.

简单句：一个主语embroidery，一个谓语由系表结构组成is time-consuming。

◎It may take a whole day to complete the length of 10 cm.

简单句：一个形式主语it，一个真正的主语to complete the length of 10 cm，一个谓语may take。

◎By the 1970s，the number of embroiderers in Sichuan had reached 5000.

简单句：一个主语number，一个谓语had reached。

◎Shu embroidery is a specialty of Chengdu，Sichuan Province.

简单句：一个主语Shu embroidery，一个谓语由系表结构组成is a specialty。

◎Shu embroidery is one of the longest handed down embroideries in China.

简单句：一个主语Shu embroidery，一个谓语is one of embroideries。

◎It spread to other countries through the Southern Silk Road.

简单句：一个主语it，一个谓语spread。

◎It is even a fashion product of ancient Rome.

简单句：一个主语it，一个谓语is a product。

◎For thousands of years，Shu embroidery has represented Sichuan culture，so we should save it.

并列句：由并列连词so把两个简单句For thousands of years，Shu embroidery has represented Sichuan culture和we should save it连在一起。

并列句点拨：除了and和but之外，当so表示"所以、因此"含义的时候，也可以作为并列连词，被用于连接两个内容上有因果、顺承关系的并列分句。

构词与常用搭配

embroidery（*n.*）刺绣品；刺绣：由前缀em-（使……）加上词根broid=braid（扭），再加上词尾-ery（表"行为"）组成。

常用搭配：hand embroidery，embroidery silk

consume（*v.*）消耗，耗费（燃料、能量、时间等）：源于拉丁语。con-表示"加强"，-sum指"拿，取"。

常用搭配：consume fuels，consume energy

length（*n.*）长度：由词根leng（=long，表示"长"）和后缀-th（表示"性质，状态"）组成。

常用搭配：maximum length，full length，same length，average length

specialty（*n.*）特产：词根special，指"特别的"，后缀-ty表示"性质，情况，状态"。

常用搭配：regional specialties，Local Specialties，Specialties Room

fashion（*n.*）（行为、活动等的）时尚，时兴：来自法语。原为faction，法语中发生音变，写成fashion。由fash-=fac-（做）加上名词词尾-ion组成。

常用搭配：follow fashion，set fashion

ancient（*a.*）古代的：由两部分组成：anci-（古老）+-ent（形容词词尾：具有……性质的，关于……的）

常用搭配：ancient city，ancient town，ancient history，ancient culture，ancient civilization

Crossword Puzzle

Across

1. to use something, especially fuel, energy or time

4. a popular way of behaving, doing an activity, etc.

6. patterns that are sewn onto cloth using threads of various colours; cloth that is decorated in this way

Down

2. special local product

3. belonging to a period of history that is thousands of years in the past

5. the size or measurement of something from one end to the other

Traditional Chinese Medicine（TCM）中医药

Nowadays，when people in western countries feel uncomfortable，they often choose to take traditional Chinese medicine（TCM）. For them，it is a new kind of medicine. As a matter of fact，traditional Chinese medicine has a long history in China and has been widely used to treat a variety of difficult and complicated diseases. Take herbal medicines，for example，they contribute to the balance of the body. In a word，a lot of treatments used in TCM have helped people in the world effectively for thousands of years.

Reading Comprehension

Background Information

中医药学是中华传统文化的宝藏，蕴含了中华民族多年以来的健康理念和丰富的实践经验。我国著名的中药学专家李时珍被称为药圣，他所著的《本草纲目》因其内容广泛、记载详尽而驰名中外。保护和传承中医药文化有助于建设健康中国，也有利于全世界人民的健康事业。

Critical Thinking

Question One：Doctors of traditional Chinese medicine pay attention to the diagnosis and treatments based on an overall analysis of the illness and the patient's condition. What do you think of the effects of their four basic diagnostic methods?

Question Two：How much do you know about Fu Xi and his invention of bagua? What is bagua's influence on Chinese philosophy? How will you understand Confucius's statement—if he could study the bagua for 50 years he might be able to obtain wisdom?

Question Three：Have you ever been to any traditional Chinese medicine hospital? Can you tell the differences between TCM and Western medicine? How do you think of the integration of TCM and Western medicine?

Language Focus

英语句子结构上具有后开放性特点，因此在使用英语表达时应该先将句子的主干提取出来，最后再添上句子的其他附加成分。

句子主干 指的是构成一个完整句子的框架，主要包括几个基本句子成分：主语、谓语、宾语、表语。

本语篇一共由5个句子构成，它们的句子主干分别是：

☆They choose.

☆It is a medicine.

☆Traditional Chinese medicine has a history and has been used.

☆They contribute to the balance.

☆Treatments have helped people.

句子附加成分 指的是去除一个完整句子中的主干部分剩余的修饰、补充说明部分，主要包括几个基本句子成分：定语、状语、宾语补足语、主语补足语、同位语、插入语。

本语篇的句子附加成分如下：

★nowadays（副词作状语）

★often （副词作状语）

★traditional（形容词作定语）

★Chinese（形容词作定语）

★for them（介词短语作状语）

★new（形容词作定语）

★of medicine（介词短语作后置定语）

★as a matter of fact（介词短语作状语）

★long（形容词作定语）

★in China（介词短语作状语）

★widely（副词作状语）

★difficult（形容词作定语）

★complicated（形容词作定语）

★take herbal medicines for example（动词原形作插入语）

★of the body（介词短语作定语）

★in a word（介词短语作状语）

★a lot of（介词短语作定语）

★in the world（介词短语作定语）

★effectively（副词作状语）

★for thousands of years（介词短语作状语）

非谓语动词 指动词在句子中不作谓语时的形式，因此它不受主语的限制。非谓语动词在英语句子中使用频繁且广泛。它可以在句子中充当除了谓语之外的其他成分，主语、宾语、表语、定语、状语、补语等。非谓语动词分为3大类：

◆动词不定式：to do / to be

◆动名词：doing / being

◆分词，一个是现在分词：doing / being；另一个是过去分词：done / been。

本语篇中非谓语动词的使用：

◇**to take** traditional Chinese medicine动词不定式短语作宾语

◇**to treat** a variety of difficult and complicated diseases动词不定式短语作目的状语

◇**used** in TCM过去分词短语作定语

句子类型 句子类型主要包括：简单句、复合句和并列句。在用英文表达时，尽量得体、恰当地交叉使用它们。简单句是指，一个主语或者两个、多个并列主语加上一个谓语或者两个、多个并列谓语构成的句子。复合句是指，一个主句加上一个或者多个从句构成的句子。并列句是指，由并列连词把两个或多个简单句连在一起构成的句子。

本语篇中句子类型的使用：

◎Nowadays，when people in western countries feel uncomfortable，they often choose to take traditional Chinese medicine（TCM）.

复合句：一个主句they often choose to take traditional Chinese medicine，一个时间状语从句when people in western countries feel uncomfortable。

◎For them，it is a new kind of medicine.

简单句：一个主语it，一个谓语is a new kind of medicine由系表结构组成。

◎As a matter of fact，traditional Chinese medicine has a long history in China and has been widely used to treat a variety of difficult and complicated diseases.

简单句：一个主语traditional Chinese medicine一个并列谓语has...and has been used.

◎Take herbal medicines for example，they contribute to the balance of the body.

简单句：一个主语they，一个谓语contribute。

◎In a word，a lot of treatments used in TCM have helped people in the world effectively for thousands of years.

简单句：一个主语treatments，一个谓语have helped。

时间状语从句点拨：用表示时间的连词连接一个句子作状语，这样的主从复合句就是时间状语从句。常见的表示时间的连接词有：after，as，before，since，till，until，when……其中由when引导的居多，有时when引导的状语从句根据具体语境也可以理解为条件状语从句，本篇章中的when people in western countries feel uncomfortable就可理解为条件状语。

构词与常用搭配

uncomfortable（*a.*）感到不舒服的：由词根fort（堡垒；力量）加上前缀com-（共同）构成comfort（安慰），再加上形容词后缀-able（能够）和否定前缀un-构成。

常用搭配：feel uncomfortable，uncomfortable shoes，uncomfortable position，uncomfortable silence，look uncomfortable

traditional（*a.*）传统的：由词根dit=give（给），加上前缀tra-=trans-=cross（交叉），即"代代相传，传承"，再加上表示名词的后缀-ion，最后加上形容词后缀-al构成。

常用搭配：traditional beliefs，traditional culture，traditional medicine，traditional method，traditional practices，traditional system，traditional style，traditional values

medicine（*n.*）医学：自拉丁语mederi（诊断，治疗），由词根med（测量，考虑，建议，采取手段，词源同 measure），加上名词词尾-ine（状态）构成。

常用搭配：Chinese medicine，clinical medicine，herbal medicine，modern medicine，preventative medicine，traditional medicine，Western medicine

variety（*n.*）多样化：由词根vary/vari=change（变化）加上名词词尾-（e）ty构成。

常用搭配：different varieties，wide variety，new variety，rare variety

complicated（*a.*）复杂的：由词根plic = fold（折叠；重复），加上前缀com-（共同），加上动词词尾-ate，再变成过去分词加-ed构成。

常用搭配：complicated case，complicated instructions，complicated plot，complicated problem，complicated process，complicated situation，complicated system

disease（*n.*）疾病：由词根eas（舒适，容易）加上否定前缀dis- 构成。

常用搭配：cause disease，chronic disease，common disease，control disease，cure disease，fatal disease，incurable disease，infectious disease，liver disease，prevent disease，rare disease，treat disease

herbal（*a.*）药草的：由词根herb（草，草药）加上形容词后缀 -al构成。

常用搭配：herbal cigarettes，herbal extract，herbal medicine，herbal remedies，herbal tea

contribute（*v.*）构成……原因：由词根tribut=give（给予）加上前缀con-（一起）构成。

常用搭配：contribute ideas，contribute share，contribute to，contribute some money

balance（*n.*）平衡：源自古拉丁语 bilanx，由词根lanx=pans（盘）加上前缀bi-=two（两个），再加上表示"物品，性质，状况"的名词后缀 -ance构成；它的本义是"天平"，即由两个秤盘构成的物品。后来逐渐衍生出"平衡"的比喻之意。

常用搭配：achieve balance，balance budget，keep balance，strike balance，lose balance，maintain balance，on balance

treatment（*n.*）治疗：由词根treat=tract（拖、拉、拽）引申为handle（处理），

加上表示名词的-ment构成。

常用搭配：soft treatment, successful treatment, preferential treatment, effective treatment, same treatment, give treatment, receive treatment, get treatment, provide treatment, undergo treatment

effectively（*adv.*）有效地：由词根fect=do / make（做,制作）加上前缀ef-=ex-（出）加上形容词后缀 -ive和副词词尾 -ly构成。

常用搭配：control effectively, manage effectively, protect effectively, run effectively, use effectively, work effectively

Crossword Puzzle

Across

1. something that is done to cure an illness or injury, or to make somebody look and feel good

3. several different sorts of the same thing

4. in a way that is successful and achieves what you want

6. involving a lot of different parts, in a way that is difficult to understand

8. not feeling physically relaxed, warm, etc.

10. treatment for illness or injury, or the study of this

11. relating to or made from herbs

Down

2. being part of the beliefs, customs or way of life of a particular group of people, that have not changed for a long time

5. a state where things are of equal weight or force

7. to be one of the causes of something

9. illness of people, animals, plants, etc., caused by infection or a failure of health rather than by an accident

Chinese Winter Solstice Culture 中国 "冬至" 文化

There are 24 solar terms according to the traditional Chinese lunar calendar. The Winter Solstice is one of them. The Winter Solstice, which is also called "Winter festival", comes on December 22nd or December 23rd. China is located in the Northern Hemisphere, and on Winter Solstice the night is the longest throughout the year. From the Winter Solstice on, the day is getting longer until the Summer Solstice and China experiences the approach of the coldest time of the year, which is known as *shu jiu*—nine periods with nine days for each. As early as in the Zhou Dynasty, a great ceremony was held to offer sacrifice to heaven on the Winter Solstice which was as significant as the New Year.

Reading Comprehension

Background Information

二十四节气是中国古代人民根据地球在黄道，即地球绕太阳公转的轨道上的位置变化规律而制定的历法，其目的是更好地农耕。它是中国古代人民长期积累下来的经验和智慧。根据太阳的运行规律而制定的二十四节气，反映出太阳运行的周期，概括了一年中不同时期太阳在黄道上的位置变化的规律、冰霜雨雪等自然现象的规律和春夏秋冬的准确时间，记载了大自然中一些物候现象的时刻。根据二十四节气古人进行农事耕作，其衣食住行，甚至是文化观念也深受其影响。

Critical Thinking

Question One: Under those simple scientific conditions, ancient Chinese people were able to identity the exact time of winter and summer. How do you think of ancient Chinese people?

Question Two: Are you in favor of keeping those eating customs on Winter Solstice? Why or why not?

Question Three: The 24 solar terms are of great significance to agriculture in China. For ordinary people living in big cities, what are the significance and functions of the 24 solar terms?

Language Focus

英语句子结构上具有后开放性特点，因此在使用英语表达时应该先将句子的主干提取出来，最后再添上句子的其他附加成分。

句子主干 指的是构成一个完整句子的框架，主要包括几个基本句子成分：主语、谓语、宾语、表语。

本语篇一共由6个句子构成，它们的句子主干分别是：

☆ There are terms.

☆ Winter Solstice is one.

☆ Winter Solstice comes.

☆ China is located.

☆ The day is getting longer.

☆ A ceremony was held.

句子附加成分 指的是去除一个完整句子中的主干部分剩余的修饰、补充说明部分，主要包括几个基本句子成分：定语、状语、宾语补足语、主语补足语、同位语、插入语。

本语篇的句子附加成分如下：

★ 24（数词作定语）

★ solar（形容词作定语）

★ according to the traditional Chinese lunar calendar（介词短语作状语）

★ of them（介词短语作后置定语）

★ which is also called "Winter festival"（非限定性定语从句）

★ on December 22nd or December 23rd（介词短语作时间状语）

★ in the Northern Hemisphere（介词短语作地点状语）

★ on Winter Solstice（介词短语作时间状语）

★ throughout the year（介词短语作时间状语）

★ From the Winter Solstice on（介词短语作时间状语）

★ until the Summer Solstice（介词短语作时间状语）

★ of the coldest period（介词短语作定语）

★ which is also called *shu jiu*—nine periods with nine days for each（非限定性定语从句）

★ As early as in the Zhou Dynasty（介词短语作时间状语）

★ to offer sacrifice to heaven（动词不定式短语作目的状语）

★on the Winter Solstice（介词短语作时间状语）

★which was as significant as the New Year（限定性定语从句）

非谓语动词 是指动词在句子中不作谓语时的形式，因此它不受主语的限制。非谓语动词在英语句子中使用频繁且广泛。它可以在句子中充当除了谓语之外的其他成分，主语、宾语、表语、定语、状语、补语等。非谓语动词分为3大类：

◆动词不定式：to do / to be

◆动名词：doing / being

◆分词，一个是现在分词：doing / being；另一个是过去分词：done / been。

本语篇中非谓语动词的使用：

◇**to offer** sacrifice to heaven on the Winter Solstice 动词不定式状语表目的。

句子类型 主要包括：简单句、复合句和并列句。在用英文表达时，尽量得体、恰当地交叉使用它们。简单句是指，一个主语或者两个、多个并列主语加上一个谓语或者两个、多个并列谓语构成的句子。复合句是指，一个主句加上一个或者多个从句构成的句子。并列句是指，由并列连词把两个或多个简单句连在一起构成的句子。

本语篇中句子类型的使用：

◎There are 24 solar terms according to the traditional Chinese lunar calendar.

简单句：there be句型，一个主语solar terms，一个谓语are。

◎The Winter Solstice is one of them.

简单句：主系表结构，一个主语The Winter Solstice，一个系动词is，一个表语one。

◎The Winter Solstice, which is also called "Winter festival", comes on December 22nd or December 23rd.

◎复合句：一个主句The Winter Solstice comes on December 22nd or December 23rd，一个从句which is also called "Winter festival"。

◎China is located in the Northern Hemisphere, and on Winter Solstice the night is the longest throughout the year.

并列句：由并列连词and连接China is located in the Northern Hemisphere和on Winter Solstice the night is the longest throughout the year两个句子。

◎From the Winter Solstice on, the day is getting longer until the Summer Solstice and China experiences the approach of the coldest time of the year, which is known as *shu jiu*——nine periods with nine days for each.

复合句：一个主句From the Winter Solstice on, the day is getting longer。

两个从句：从句一是时间状语从句until the Summer Solstice and China experiences the approach of the coldest time of the year，而且该从句中还含有并列连词and连接的并列句China experiences the approach of the coldest time of the year；

从句二是非限定性定语从句which is also called *shu jiu*——nine periods with nine days for each

◎As early as in the Zhou Dynasty, a great ceremony was held to offer sacrifice to heaven on the Winter Solstice which was as significant as the New Year.

复合句：一个主句As early as in the Zhou Dynasty, a great ceremony was held to offer sacrifice to heaven on the Winter Solstice.

一个从句 which was as significant as the New Year

错综复合句点拨：错综复合句是句子既包含复合句，又有并列句的杂糅复杂句。分析清楚句子之间的逻辑关系是从属关系还是同等并列关系就能将顺它的句意。

构词与常用搭配

calendar（*n.*）日历：源自拉丁语中表示"罗马月份的第一天"的单词。

常用搭配：solar calendar, lunar calendar, Chinese calendar

solstice（*n.*）至点，夏至或冬至：由词根sol（太阳）加上词根 -st（站住，停止，词源同 stand-）加上名词后缀-ice构成。字面意思即太阳停止的地方，用于指夏至（北回归线）或冬至（南回归线）。

常用搭配：winter solstice, summer solstice

locate（*v.*）位于：由词根locus（地点）加上动词后缀 -ate构成。引申词义"定位"。

常用搭配：be located in, locate mode, locate file

hemisphere（*n.*）半球：由前缀hemi-（半）加上词根词sphere（球）构成。

常用搭配：Eastern Hemisphere, Southern Hemisphere, dominant hemisphere

approach（*n.*）接近：由词根源于一个拉丁语词，表示proach=prope（接近）加上前缀ap=ad（去）构成。

常用搭配：cautious approach，an approach to，design approach

dynasty（n.）朝代：来自希腊语 dynamis，力量，权力，统治者。引申词义朝代

常用搭配：Qing Dynasty，Tudor Dynasty，Jade Dynasty

sacrifice（n.）祭品：由词根sacri（与sacred神的同源）加上后缀-fice（与词根fact 做，从事同源）构成，因此从字面意思理解sacrifice就是"为神做的事"。

常用搭配：human sacrifice，sacrifice hit，soul sacrifice

Crossword Puzzle

Across

2. the act of drawing spatially closer to something
6. determine or indicate the place, site, or limits of, as if by an instrument or by a survey
7. the offering of food, objects or the lives of animals to a higher purpose, in particular divine beings, as an act of propitiation

Down

1. a sequence of powerful leaders in the same family
3. half of the terrestrial globe
4. either of the two times of the year when the sun is at its greatest distance from the celestial equator
5. a system of timekeeping that defines the beginning and length and divisions of the year

Ethnic Culture 民族文化

China is a multi-ethnic country united by the Chinese civilization. Since ancient times, China has been a multi-ethnic country. There are 56 ethnic groups officially identified by government's investigation and statistics. In accordance with the data of the seventh national census in 2020, the Han ethnic group accounts for the largest one with 91.11% of the total national population. The second is the Zhuang ethnic minority and Gaoshan ethinic minority has the least number of people. The distribution of the various ethnic groups in China is featured by living together in large or small communities, other provinces or municipalities.

Reading Comprehension

Background Information

自古以来中国就拥有很多个民族。几千年来分裂与融合在众多民族间不断上演，这期间各民族形成了各自独特的语言与风俗习惯。古人最初按照生活的区域来划分不同的族群，到了唐代，民族这一概念第一次被唐太宗提出。1953年新中国进行第一次人口普查时，以语言和文化两个特点来划分不同的民族。这一方法非常的科学，也更加标准。在1954年确立了最初的39个民族。后来经过几十年的变迁，又有17个少数民族融合进来，至此形成了现在的56个民族。

Critical Thinking

Question One: In the context of globalization, what is the significance of preserving ethnic languages and customs? What's your opinion on "the more national, the more global"?

Question Two: How can the living habits, customs and languages of various ethnic groups be preserved?

Question Three: Do you wholeheartedly approve of cultural diversity with ethnic groups and the coexixtence of several cultures in one world?

Language Focus

英语句子结构上具有后开放性特点，因此在使用英语表达时应该先将句子的主干提取出来，最后再添上句子的其他附加成分。

句子主干 指的是构成一个完整句子的框架，主要包括几个基本句子成分：主语、谓语、宾语、表语。

本语篇一共由6个句子构成，它们的句子主干分别是：

☆China is a country.

☆China has been a country.

☆There are groups.

☆Han accounts for one.

☆Second is Zhuang and Gaoshan has number.

☆The distribution is featured.

句子附加成分 指的是去除一个完整句子中的主干部分剩余的修饰、补充说明部分，主要包括几个基本句子成分：定语、状语、宾语补足语、主语补足语、同位语、插入语。

本语篇的句子附加成分如下：

★multi-ethnic（形容词作定语）

★united by the Chinese civilization（过去分词短语作后置定语）

★Since ancient times（介词短语作时间状语）

★56（数词作定语）

★ethnic（形容词作定语）

★officially（副词作状语）

★identified（动词过去式作后置定语）

★by government's investigation and statistics（由介词by引导的介词短语在被动语态句子中引出施动者）

★In accordance with the data of the seventh national census in 2020（介词短语作方式状语）

★largest（形容词作定语）

★with 91.11% of the total national population（介词短语作后置定语）

★the least number of（名词短语作定语）

★of the various ethnic groups（介词短语作定语）

★in China（介词短语作地点状语）

★by living together in large or small communities（介词短语作状语）

★in autonomous regions，other provinces or municipalities（介词短语作状语）

非谓语动词 是指动词在句子中不作谓语时的形式，因此它不受主语的限制。非谓语动词在英语句子中使用频繁且广泛。它可以在句子中充当除了谓语之外的其他成分，主语、宾语、表语、定语、状语、补语等。非谓语动词分为3大类：

◆动词不定式：to do / to be

◆动名词：doing / being

◆分词，一个是现在分词：doing / being；另一个是过去分词：done / been。

本语篇中非谓语动词的使用：

◇a multi-ethnic country **united** by the Chinese civilization 过去分词作定语表示的含义有被动、完成。

◇56 ethnic groups officially **identified** by government's investigation and statistics 过去分词作定语表示的含义有被动、完成。

句子类型 主要包括：简单句、复合句和并列句。在用英文表达时，尽量得体、恰当地交叉使用它们。简单句是指，一个主语或者两个、多个并列主语加上一个谓语或者两个、多个并列谓语构成的句子。复合句是指，一个主句加上一个或者多个从句构成的句子。并列句是指，由并列连词把两个或多个简单句连在一起构成的句子。

本语篇中句子类型的使用：

◎China is a multi-ethnic country united by the Chinese civilization.

简单句：主系表结构，一个主语China，一个系动词is，一个表语是country。

◎Since ancient times, China has been a multi-ethnic country.

简单句：一个主语China，一个谓语has been。

◎There are 56 ethnic groups officially identified by government's investigation and statistics.

简单句：there be句型，一个主语groups，一个谓语 are。

◎In accordance with the data of the seventh national census in 2020, the Han ethnic group accounts for the largest one with 91.11% of the total national population.

简单句：一个主语the Han ethnic group，一个谓语accounts for。

◎The second is the Zhuang ethnic minority and Gaoshan ethnic minority has the least number of people.

并列句：由连词and把两个简单句The second is the Zhuang ethnic minority和Gaoshan ethnic minority has the least number of people连接在一起。

◎The distribution of the various ethnic groups in China is featured by living together in large or small communities in autonomous regions，other provinces or municipalities.

简单句：一个主语The distribution，一个谓语is featured。

并列句点拨：判断并列句的关键是并列连词，连词有表达联合、转折和因果等不同的作用。

如，连词and表达顺承或并列关系。并列句，尤其是表达顺承和转折的并列句在英文表达中使用频率较高。

构词与常用搭配

ancient（a.）古代的：源于拉丁语副词ante（前，过去）。由词根anci（ance-前）加上形容词后缀 -ent 构成。

常用搭配：Ancient Greece，in ancient times，Ancient Rome

identify（v.）确认、辨认：由词根 -ident-（相同）加上后缀 -ify（使成为）构成。

常用搭配：identify oneself，identify with，identify root cause

investigation（n.）调查：它的动词investigate源自拉丁文 investigare，前缀in=into（循着）加上词根vestigate（源自vestigium 表示脚印、痕迹，引申为跟踪），和名词后缀-tion构成，字面意思就是"循着脚印跟踪、探究"。

常用搭配：under investigation，on the spot investigation，field investigation

community（n.）群体：前缀com-（共同）加词根-mun-（公共）和名词后缀 -ity 构成。

常用搭配：virtual community，Asian Community，community college

minority（n.）少数民族：由词根 minor（较小的，较少的）加上名词后缀-ity构成。引申词义少数派，少数民族。

常用搭配：be in a/the minority，minority group，minority opinion

autonomous（a.）自治的：由前缀auto-（源于希腊语autos 自己）加上词根nom（希腊语、法则，秩序）和形容词后缀-ous构成。

常用搭配：autonomous region，autonomous county，autonomous system

Crossword Puzzle

Across

2. a group of people living in a particular local area

3. of many different kinds purposefully arranged but lacking any uniformity

7. giving or be given to each of several people

8. to recognize someone and be able to tell who they are

Down

1. (of political bodies) not controlled by outside forces

4. belonging to times long past

5. a branch of applied mathematics concerned with the collection and interpretation of quantitative data and the use of probability

6. a group of people who differ racially or politically from a larger group of which it is a part

Yangtze River Culture 长江文化

Yangtze River, the largest river in China, has played a vital role in the origin and development of Chinese civilization. China plans to construct national parks with Yangtze River culture as their theme and China will make efforts to preserve the waterway's cultural heritage, built the spiritual home of the Chinese nation and present the colorful Chinese civilization to the world. A circular on promoting the parks' construction issued by the central leading group shows that the parks will be located in the 13 provincial-level regions in the Yangtze basin and the leading group for the construction of national cultural parks will strengthen overall planning and coordination to ensure high-quality progress in the construction.

Reading Comprehension

Background Information

在漫长的历史长河中，因居民的生活习惯、语言文化、传统习俗的不同而衍生出了黄河文化和长江文化两种最具代表性的文化形式。其中，长江文化是一种以长江流域的主要地理特征为主导，结合当地人文、生产活动、社会结构，以及生产力发展水平为基础的文化体系；也是最能代表和影响中华文明的核心文化之一。长江文化融合了长江流域各民族的文化成就，是南方文化体系中最重要的一环。

Critical Thinking

Question One: How can the Yangtze River cultural heritages be well preserved?

Question Two: During the construction of Yangtze River cultural parks, what measures should be taken to protect both the ecology and traditional cultures?

Question Three: Have you heard of Disneyland Theme Park, and have you been there? What is your opinion on the Yangtze River National Cultural Park? What are the differences between them in terms of culture international communication?

Language Focus

英语句子结构上具有后开放性特点，因此，在使用英语表达时应该先将句子的主干提取出来，最后再添上句子的其他附加成分。

句子主干 指的是构成一个完整句子的框架，主要包括主语、谓语、宾语、表语等基本句子成分。

本语篇一共由3个句子构成，它们的句子主干分别是：

☆Yangtze River has played a role.

☆China plans to construct national parks and China will make efforts.

☆A circular shows.

句子附加成分 指的是去除一个完整句子中的主干部分剩余的修饰、补充说明部分，主要包括定语、状语、宾语补足语、主语补足语、同位语、插入语这几个基本句子成分。

本语篇的句子附加成分如下：

★the largest river（名词短语作同位语）

★in China（介词短语作后置定语）

★vital（形容词作定语）

★in the origin and development（介词短语作状语）

★of Chinese civilization（介词短语作后置定语）

★with Yangtze River culture（介词短语作定语）

★as their theme（介词短语作状语）

★to preserve cultural heritage（不定式作目的状语）

★the river's（名词所有格作定语）

★Chinese（形容词作定语）

★to the world（介词短语作状语）

★on promoting construction（介词短语作定语）

★the parks'（名词所有格作定语）

★issued by the group（过去分词作定语）

★central（形容词作定语）

★leading（形容词作定语）

★in the 13 regions（介词短语作状语）

★provincial-level（名词词组作定语）

★for the construction（介词短语作定语）

★in the Yangtze basin（介词短语作定语）

★of national cultural parks（介词短语作定语）

★overall（形容词作定语）

★to ensure progress（不定式作目的状语）

★high-quality（名词词组作定语）

★in the construction（介词短语作状语）

非谓语动词 是指动词形式有一定的变换，在句子中不作谓语，因此，它不受主语的限制。非谓语动词在英语中很常见。它可以在句子中充当主语、宾语、表语、定语、状语、补语等句子成分。非谓语动词有以下三种形式：

◆动词不定式：to do / to be

◆动名词：doing / being

◆分词，一个是现在分词：doing / being；另一个是过去分词：done / been。

本语篇中非谓语动词的使用：

◇**issued** by the central leading group过去分词短语作后置定语，表示的含义有被动、完成。

◇**to preserve** the waterway's cultural heritage，**built** the spiritual home of the Chinese nation and **present** the colorful Chinese civilization to the world 不定式作目的状语，表示的含义有动作的目的。

句子类型 主要包括简单句、复合句和并列句。在用英文表达时，尽量得体、恰当地交叉使用它们。简单句是指，一个主语或者两个以上主语加上一个谓语或者两个以上谓语构成的句子。复合句是指，一个主句加上一个或者多个从句构成的句子。并列句是指，两个以上简单句由并列连词连在一起构成的句子。

本语篇中句子类型的使用：

◎Yangtze River，the largest river in China，has played a vital role in the origin and development of Chinese civilization.

简单句：一个主语Yangtze River，一个谓语has played，一个宾语a vital role。

◎China plans to construct national parks with Yangtze River culture as their theme and China will make efforts to preserve the waterway's cultural heritage，built the spiritual home of the Chinese nation and present the colorful Chinese civilization to the world.

并列句：由并列连词and连接两个简单句，简单句一China plans to construct national park with Yangtze River culture as their theme；简单句二China will make efforts to preserve the waterway's cultural heritage，built the spiritual home of the Chinese nation and present the colorful Chinese civilization to the world。

简单句二中又含有并列连词and连接的同一个主语的三个不同并列谓语：will make efforts，built和present。

◎A circular on promoting the parks' construction issued by the central leading group shows that the parks will be located in the 13 provincial-level regions in the Yangtze basin and the leading group for the construction of national cultural parks will strengthen overall planning and coordination to ensure high-quality progress in the construction.

复合句：一个主句A circular shows，一个从句由that 引导句子the parks will be located in the 13 provincial-level regions in the Yangtze basin and the leading group for the construction of national cultural parks will strengthen overall planning and coordination to ensure high-quality progress in the construction 作宾语。

宾语从句又包含由并列连词and连接的两个并列分句：the parks will be located in the 13 provincial-level regions in the Yangtze basin和the leading group for the construction of national cultural parks will strengthen overall planning and coordination to ensure high-quality progress in the construction。

错综复合句点拨：从句在整个复合句中充当什么句子成分就是什么从句。例如，宾语从句就是该从句在整个复合句中作宾语成分。从句里如果再含有并列句就构成错综复合句。虽然结构比较复杂，错综复合句在英文表达中使用也很多。

构词与常用搭配

vital（*a.*）必不可少的：由vit-活+-al 形容词词尾构成。

常用搭配：vital people/organ/clues/issues

origin（*n.*）起源：源自一个拉丁语词表示"升起，上升"，后来引申为"起源"。

常用搭配：country of origin，origin of life，ethic origion

civilization（*n.*）文明：由civil 公民的+-zation名词词尾构成。

常用搭配：progress and civilization，world civilization

construct（*v.*）建造：由con-加强意义+-struct建设、结构构成。

常用搭配：construct a plan，construct a belief，construct a model

preserve（*v.*）保护：由pre-前，先+-serv-保持，留心+-e动词词尾构成。

常用搭配：preserve the environment，preserve the character，preserved the right

heritage（*n.*）遗产：由herit-继承+-age构成。

常用搭配：cultural heritage，world heritage site

circular（*n.*）通知：由circ-圆+-ular 形容词词尾构成。

常用搭配：court circular，an urgent circular

issue（*v.*）发布：源自古法语、拉丁语表示"出口，出去"的词，后引申为出版、发行、期刊等。

常用搭配：at issue，take issue with

strengthen（*v.*）加强：由strength力量+-en动词词尾构成。

常用搭配：strengthened belief，strengthen the position

coordination（*n.*）协调：由co-共同+-ordin-秩序，顺序+-ation名词词尾构成。

常用搭配：in coordination with，coordination ability

Crossword Puzzle

Across

3. a letter or notice sent to a large number of people

7. the act of making all the people involved in a plan or activity work together in an organized way

8. a subject or problem that people are thinking and talking about

9. to make something stronger or more effective, or to become stronger or more effective

10. features belonging to the culture of a particular society, such as traditions, languages, or buildings, that were created in the past and still have historical importance

Down

1. necessary for the success or continued existence of something; extremely important

2. human society with its well developed social organizations, or the culture and way of life of a society or country at a particular period in time

4. to keep something as it is, especially in order to prevent it from decaying or being damaged or destroyed

5. the beginning or cause of something

6. to build something or put together different parts to form something whole

A Bite of China 舌尖上的中国

Chinese cuisine is famous and favored all over the world. The simple categories of Chinese cuisine include the following eight kinds: Lu, Chuan, Yue, Su, Min, Zhe, Xiang and Hui cuisine. Lu, Chuan and Yue cuisines are the most distinctive ones. The food in Lu cuisine incorporates materials, such as domestic animals and birds, seafood and vegetables. The features are salty and fresh usually with good use of scallion and garlic. Chuan cuisine is famous for the bold flavors of pungency and spiciness and it is mainly because of the usage of garlic and chili peppers. Yue food consists of a wide range of raw materials, from common materials to special ones such as offal, duck's tongue and snakes.

Reading Comprehension

Background Information

中国有五千年的文明史，也有来自五湖四海触动人们神经和味蕾的山珍美味，令人垂涎。不同的地区，由于气候、地理和物产的不同，在漫长演变中，形成自成一派的独特烹饪技术和风味。中国人餐桌上的食物原料以植物性食物为主，主食是五谷，菜以蔬菜和肉食为主。食用热食和熟食，也是中国饮食的一大特点。中国有着非常发达的烹饪技术，煎炒烹炸闷溜熬炖，种类繁多。同一种食材，用不同的烹饪技术，能做出几十种味道。烹调技术高超，令人赞叹。

Critical Thinking

Question One: Can you introduce your local cuisine? What will you highly recommend in the menu for the New Year's feast?

Question Two: Chinese medicine emphasizes the medicinal function of food—a healing cuisine. Do you have any special eating habit according to your health condition to regulate your body? What healing cuisine will you introduce?

Question Three: What's the relation between cuisine features and the climate?

Language Focus

英语句子结构上具有后开放性特点，因此在使用英语表达时应该先将句子的主干提取出来，最后再添上句子的其他附加成分。

句子主干 指的是构成一个完整句子的框架，主要包括几个基本句子成分：主语、谓语、宾语、表语。

本语篇一共由7个句子构成，它们的句子主干分别是：

☆Chinese cuisine is famous and favored.

☆Categories includes kinds.

☆Lu，Chuan and Yue cuisines are ones.

☆The food incorporates materials.

☆The features are salty and fresh.

☆Chuan cuisine is famous and it is because of the usage.

☆Yue food uses materials.

句子附加成分 指的是去除一个完整句子中的主干部分剩余的修饰、补充说明部分，主要包括几个基本句子成分：定语、状语、宾语补足语、主语补足语、同位语、插入语。

本语篇的句子附加成分如下：

★all over the world（介词短语作地点状语）

★simple（形容词作定语）

★of Chinese cuisine（介词短语作后置定语）

★the following eight（形容词短语作定语）

★Lu，Chuan，Yue，Su，Min，Zhe，Xiang and Hui cuisine（名词短语作补语）

★the most distinctive（形容词短语作定语）

★in Lu cuisine（介词短语作后置定语）

★such as domestic animals and birds，seafood and vegetables（名词短语作补语）

★usually（副词作状语）

★with good use of scallion and garlic（介词短语作状语）

★for the bold flavors of pungency（介词短语作状语）

★mainly（副词作状语）

★of garlic and chili peppers（介词短语作后置定语）

★a wide range of（名词短语作定语）

★from common materials to special ones such as offal，duck's tongue and snakes（介词短语作补语）

非谓语动词 是指动词在句子中不作谓语时的形式，因此它不受主语的限制。非谓语动词在英语句子中使用频繁且广泛。它可以在句子中充当除了谓语之外的其他成分，主语、宾语、表语、定语、状语、补语等。非谓语动词分为3大类：

◆ 动词不定式：to do / to be

◆ 动名词：doing / being

◆ 分词，一个是现在分词：doing / being；另一个是过去分词：done / been。

本语篇中非谓语动词的使用：

◇ the **following** eight kinds现在分词作定语表示动作的进行、主动。

句子类型 主要包括：简单句、复合句和并列句。在用英文表达时，尽量得体、恰当地交叉使用它们。简单句是指，一个主语或者两个、多个并列主语加上一个谓语或者两个、多个并列谓语构成的句子。复合句是指，一个主句加上一个或者多个从句构成的句子。并列句是指，由并列连词把两个或多个简单句连在一起构成的句子。

本语篇中句子类型的使用：

◎ Chinese cuisine is famous and favored all over the world.

简单句：主系表结构，一个主语Chinese cuisine，一个系动词is。

◎ The simple categories of Chinese cuisine include the following eight kinds：Lu, Chuan, Yue, Su, Min, Zhe, Xiang and Hui cuisine.

简单句：一个主语The categories，一个谓语include。

◎ Lu, Chuan and Yue cuisines are the most distinctive ones.

简单句：主系表结构，三个并列主语Lu, Chuan和Yue cuisines，一个系动词are。

◎ The food in Lu cuisine incorporates materials, such as domestic animals and birds, seafood and vegetables.

简单句：一个主语The food，一个谓语incorporates。

◎ The features are salty and fresh usually with good use of scallion and garlic.

简单句：一个主语The features，一个谓语are。

◎ Chuan cuisine is famous for the bold flavors of pungency and spiciness and it is mainly because of the usage of garlic and chili peppers.

并列句：由并列连词and把两个简单句Chuan cuisine is famous for the bold flavors of pungency and spiciness和 it is mainly because of the usage of garlic and chili peppers连

在一起。

◎Yue food uses a wide range of raw materials, from common materials to special ones such as offal, duck's tongue, frog legs and snakes.

简单句：一个主语Yue food，一个谓语consists of。

简单句点拨：有理解难度的简单句是在主谓之间增添了较多附加成分。如，主语较长，这种情况就需要分析句子成分，抓住主干，找到这个较长主语的关键词，再将谓语的核心词找出来，这样主谓逻辑关系才能清晰，化繁为简、明确句子含义。主谓分离的简单句在英文表达中使用频率较高。

构词与常用搭配

category（n.）种类、范畴：该词源于古希腊，哲学家亚里士多德提出了"范畴" kategoria 来这个术语。它由kata（=cata，表示down to 或against）+agoreuein（当众宣称）构成。

常用搭配：category theory, concrete category, concrete category

include（v.）包含：该词由前缀in-（向内）加上词根 -clud-（关，闭）和动词后缀 -e 构成。

常用搭配：products include, file include

distinctive（a.）有特色的：由前缀di-（分离）加上词根 -stinct-（刺）和形容词后缀-ive构成。含义为以刺的记号表示区分。

常用搭配：distinctive feature, clear and distinctive, distinctive competence

incorporate（v.）吸收、并入：由前缀 in-（入）加上词根 -corpor-（体）和动词后缀-ate 构成。表示使并入一体。

常用搭配：incorporate a business, incorporate combine, to incorporate

domestic（a.）国内的，家里面的：改词来自拉丁语 domus（家）的。同源词有 dame, daunt, tame, timber

常用搭配：domestic violence, domestic rabbit, domestic flight

scallion（n.）香葱、大葱：来自通俗拉丁语escalonia。

常用搭配：scallion cake, spare-ribs with scallion, chicken in scallion oil

garlic（n.）大蒜：源于古英语garleac，由 gar（spear, 矛）和 leac（leek, 韭葱）组合而成。

常用搭配：garlic flavor，garlic press，garlic bulb

Crossword Puzzle

Across

2. a collection of things sharing a common attribute

5. of a feature that helps to distinguish a person or thing

Down

1. include or contain；have as a component

3. the practice or manner of preparing food or the food so prepared

4. of concern to or concerning the internal affairs of a nation；of or relating to the home

Section B   Module Project：Global Issues Discussion

传播好中国声音、在国际对话中为中国争取平等话语权的国际传播能力构建，需要我们在对外交流中充满文化自信。自信源于我们能够用英文介绍中国文化和国情。作为懂外语的中国人，你是否准备好了向世界积极传播中国文化、中国国情，为构成国际传播矩阵贡献自己的一分力量？

Short Video Project：Today，China's traditional culture is moving towards the whole society in a state of keeping pace with the times, and the new culture is emerging. Could you make them short videos and then post these videos on websites to communicate Chinese culture with confidence to the world?

Section C   Learners' Presentation

The Tiger in Chinese Culture
中国"虎"文化

Chinese Calligraphy
书法文化

如何创作具有国际传播效能的英文微视频呢？首先，创作题材要贴近受众者的喜好，尽力创制本土化微视频。更要追求英文字幕的简洁，在视频节奏调整上用拉长画面的技巧；制作节奏更均匀的视频，使得英文为母语的受众能在情感上产生共鸣。英国著名导演柯文思认为，以上英文字幕制作技巧源于汉语是一种极其简洁的语言。其次，丰富的短视频议题必将为塑造立体、全面、真实的中国形象开辟新境界。另外，短视频的设计不仅要传递表层信息，更要创新信息—情感—意义由表及里的传播路径。

Section D   Reflective Assessment

成长档案袋

	Y	N	Achievements
Am I satisfied with my project products?			
Shall I further improve my project products?			
Are my project products popular online?			
Can I communicate Chinese culture with confidence to the world?			
Have I mastered the vocabulary, sentence patterns and some background information on Chinese culture?			

Module Three

What Will You Do to Facilitate Green Development?

你将如何助力绿色发展？

　　《山里人家》正在浣洗衣服的姑娘们及她们甜美笑声的质朴力量，充满了对生活的创造力。油画从可感的"绿色生命"色彩中把我们引入抽象的生命哲思"绿水青山就是金山银山"，保护好我们的环境是千秋万代的大事。（艺术评论家王健）

　　The simple charms of the girls washing clothes and their sweet laughter are full of creativity for life. The truly tangible color of "green life" in the painting makes spectators immersed in thought of the philosophy of life that "lucid waters and lush mountains are invaluable assets", and environmental protection is a great cause to be passed down from generation to generation. (Art critic：WANG Jian)

Section A　Interpretive Input

Green Development of Yangtze River Economic Belt 长江经济带的绿色发展

During the development of the Yangtze River Economic Belt, the ecological restoration and protection is prioritized. Cities along the Yangtze River Economic Belt are making breakthroughs between green development plans while making productive economic achievements. The Yangtze River Economic Belt consists of 11 provinces and municipalities, taking up about half of China's population and contributing more than 40 percent of the country's GDP. To make sustainable development in Yangtze River Economic Belt, more efforts should be made in terms of scientific ecological promotion.

Reading Comprehension

Background Information

作为以效率、和谐、持续为目标的经济和社会发展方式，长江经济带的许多地区依托绿色的理念和内涵发展绿色产业。在经济社会发展取得成就的同时，生态环境也发生了转变。在江岸上，大片梅花竞相盛开，春意盎然。到江边看江豚、赏梅花成了当下最热门的话题。"滨江不见江，近水不亲水"，像这样的场景，在整个长江沿线比比皆是。

Critical Thinking

Question One：Why should ecological restoration and protection be prioritized? Are you in favor of that?

Question Two：What efforts should be made to make effective, sustainable and high-quality ecological construction?

Question Three：How is the balance between economic development and the construction of ecological environment kept?

Language Focus

英语句子结构上具有后开放性特点，因此，在使用英语表达时应该先将句子的主干提取出来，最后再添上句子的其他附加成分。

句子主干 指的是构成一个完整句子的框架，主要包括主语、谓语、宾语、表语等基本句子成分。

本语篇一共由4个句子构成，它们的句子主干分别是：

☆ Restoration and protection is prioritized.

☆ Cities are making breakthroughs.

☆ The Yangtze River Economic Belt consists of 11 provinces and municipalities.

☆ Efforts should be made.

句子附加成分 指的是去除一个完整句子中的主干部分剩余的修饰、补充说明部分，主要包括定语、状语、宾语补足语、主语补足语、同位语、插入语这几个基本句子成分。

本语篇的句子附加成分如下：

★ during the development（介词短语作状语）

★ of the Yangtze River Economic Belt（介词短语作后置定语）

★ ecological（形容词作定语）

★ along the Yangtze River Economic Belt（介词短语作后置定语）

★ between plans（介词短语作后置定语）

★ green（形容词作定语）

★ development（名词作定语）

★ while making achievements（从句作时间状语）

★ productive（形容词作定语）

★ economic（形容词作定语）

★ taking up...and contributing...（现在分词作伴随状语）

★ about（副词作状语）

★ of population（介词短语作后置定语）

★ China's（名词所有格作定语）

★ more than（形容词词组作定语）

★ of GDP（介词短语作后置定语）

★ the country's（名词所有格作定语）

★ sustainable（形容词作定语）

★scientific（形容词作定语）

★in Yangtze River Economic Belt（介词短语作后置定语）

★more（形容词作定语）

★in terms of promotion（介词短语作状语）

非谓语动词 是指动词形式有一定的变换，在句子中不作谓语，因此它不受主语的限制。非谓语动词在英语中很常见。它可以在句子中充当主语、宾语、表语、定语、状语、补语等句子成分。非谓语动词有以下三种形式：

◆动词不定式：to do / to be

◆动名词：doing / being

◆分词，一个是现在分词：doing / being；另一个是过去分词：done / been。

本语篇中非谓语动词的使用：

◇**taking up** about half of China's population and **contributing** more than 40 percent of the country's GDP 现在分词短语作状语，表示主动和伴随的动作。

◇**to make** sustainable development in Yangtze River Economic Belt 不定式作状语，表示目的。

句子类型 主要包括简单句、复合句和并列句。在用英文表达时，尽量得体、恰当地交叉使用它们。简单句是指，一个主语或者两个以上主语加上一个谓语或者两个以上谓语构成的句子。复合句是指，一个主句加上一个或者多个从句构成的句子。并列句是指，两个以上简单句由并列连词连在一起构成的句子。

本语篇中句子类型的使用：

◎In a meeting about the development of the Yangtze River Economic Belt，the ecological restoration and protection of the river is prioritized.

简单句：一个主语restoration and protection，一个谓语is prioritized。

◎Cities along the Yangtze River Economic Belt are making breakthroughs between green development plans while making productive economic achievements.

复合句：一个主句Economic Belt are making breakthroughs，一个从句while making productive economic achievements。

◎The Yangtze River Economic Belt consists of 11 provinces and municipalities，taking up about half of China's population and contributing more than 40 percent of the country's

GDP.

简单句：一个主语Economic Belt，一个谓语consists of。

◎To make sustainable development in Yangtze River Economic Belt，more efforts should be made in terms of scientific and high-quality ecological promotion.

简单句：一个主语more efforts，一个谓语should be made。

主从复合句点拨：从句在整个复合句中充当什么句子成分就是什么从句。例如，时间状语从句就是该从句在整个复合句中作状语成分，修饰谓语动词，表示动作发生的时间。时间状语从句在英文表达中也会频繁出现。

构词与常用搭配

ecological（a.）生态的：由eco-生态+-log-说+-ical形容词词尾构成。

常用搭配：ecological balance，ecological protection，ecological economy

restoration（n.）修复：由re-再+store贮备+-ation名词词尾构成。

常用搭配：restoration work，environmental restoration，full restoration

prioritize（v.）确定优先次序，该词来自 priority优先权，-ize使。

常用搭配：a prioritized list，prioritize tasks

breakthrough（n.）突破：由break破+through通过构成。

常用搭配：make a breakthrough，breakthrough agreement

productive（a.）富有成效的：由pro-前+-duct-引导+-ive形容词词尾构成。

常用搭配：a productive meeting，a productive relationship，productive force

consist（v.）由……组成：由con-共同+-sist站立→站在一起，并存构成。

常用搭配：consist of，consist in

municipality（n.）自治市：词根municipal源自一个拉丁语词表示"自治镇公民"，由原义古罗马公民享有的按照自己的法律管理自治镇而引申为通用化的"市政的"，再加上名词后缀-ty构成。

常用搭配：local municipality

contribute（v.）贡献：由con-加强意义+-tribut-交给+-e动词词尾构成。

常用搭配：contribute to，contributing factor

sustainable（a.）可持续的：由sus-下+-tain-握，持有+-able构成。

常用搭配：sustainable development，sustainable tool

promotion（*n.*）促进：由pro-前+-mot-移动+-ion名词词尾构成。

常用搭配：promotion prospect，sales promotion

Crossword Puzzle

Across

2. the act of encouraging something to happen or develop
4. to decide which of a group of things are the most important so that you can deal with them first
6. to be made of or formed from something
8. an important discovery or event that helps to improve a situation or provide an answer to a problem
9. having positive results
10. relating to ecology or the environment

Down

1. to give something, especially money, in order to provide or achieve something together with other people
3. a city or town with its own local government, or the local government itself
5. the act or process of returning something to its earlier good condition or position
7. able to continue over a period of time

106

An Economic Structure Facilitating Green, Low-Carbon and Circular Development 助力绿色、低碳、循环发展的经济结构

Economic development is coordinated with eco-environmental protection, which features increased production, higher living standards and healthy ecosystems. Building an eco-civilization and promoting green, low-carbon and circular development will meet people's growing demand for a pleasant environment, and will support fairer and safer development that is of higher quality, more efficient and more sustainable.

Reading Comprehension

Background Information

在过去的几十年中，尽管我国经济增长速度很快，但是生态环境却不断恶化。绿色低碳循环发展这种新的生产生活方式尊重自然、保护自然的可持续发展理念必定能助推可持续性的经济发展。目前，我国已进入经济转型升级、提高效率、增进技术的关键时期，绿色低碳循环发展这种新的生产生活方式成了现代化高质量经济体系的必由之路。为了满足人们对美好环境日益增长的需求，我们应该坚定不移地落实安全、公平的可持续发展观，合理利用资源、控制碳排放量以促进高质量高效率的发展。

Critical Thinking

Question One: Why should green, low-carbon and circular development be promoted?

Question Two: How can we live a low-carbon life? Are you willing to actively participate in and support green and low-carbon development?

Question Three: In a long run term, what can the whole world benefit from the low-carbon circular development?

Language Focus

英语句子结构上具有后开放性特点，因此在使用英语表达时应该先将句子的主干提取出来，最后再添上句子的其他附加成分。

句子主干 指的是构成一个完整句子的框架，主要包括主语、谓语、宾语、表语等基本句子成分。

本语篇一共由2个句子构成，它们的句子主干分别是：

☆Development is coordinated with protection.

☆Building an eco-civilization and promoting development will meet demand.

句子附加成分 指的是去除一个完整句子中的主干部分剩余的修饰、补充说明部分，主要包括定语、状语、宾语补足语、主语补足语、同位语、插入语这几个基本句子成分。

本语篇的句子附加成分如下：

★economic（形容词作定语）

★eco-environmental（形容词作定语）

★increased（过去分词作定语）

★higher（形容词比较级作定语）

★living（形容词作定语）

★healthy（形容词作定语）

★which features production, living standards and ecosystems（非限制性定语从句作定语）

★green（形容词作定语）

★low-carbon（形容词作定语）

★circular（形容词作定语）

★people's（名词所有格作定语）

★growing（现在分词作定语）

★for environment（介词短语作定语）

★pleasant（形容词作定语）

★fairer and safer（比较级作定语）

★of higher quality（介词短语作表语）

★more efficient（形容词比较级作表语）

★more sustainable（形容词比较级作表语）

非谓语动词 是指动词形式有一定的变换，在句子中不作谓语，因此它不受主语的限制。非谓语动词在英语中很常见。它可以在句子中充当主语、宾语、表语、定语、状语、补语等句子成分。非谓语动词有以下三种形式：

◆动词不定式：to do / to be

◆动名词：doing / being

◆分词，一个是现在分词：doing / being；另一个是过去分词：done / been。

本语篇中非谓语动词的使用：

◇**building** an eco-civilization and **promoting** green, low-carbon and circular development 现在分词短语作主语

◇**increased** production 过去分词作定语，表示完成、被动的含义

◇**growing** demand 现在分词作定语，表示进行、主动的含义

句子类型 主要包括简单句、复合句和并列句。在用英文表达时，尽量得体、恰当地交叉使用它们。简单句是指，一个主语或者两个以上主语加上一个谓语或者两个以上谓语构成的句子。复合句是指，一个主句加上一个或者多个从句构成的句子。并列句是指，两个以上简单句由并列连词连在一起构成的句子。

本语篇中句子类型的使用：

◎Economic development is coordinated with eco-environmental protection, which features increased production, higher living standards and healthy ecosystems.

复合句：一个主句 Economic development is coordinated with eco-environmental protection，一个从句which features increased production, higher living standards and healthy ecosystems。

◎Building an eco-civilization and promoting green, low-carbon and circular development will meet people's growing demand for a pleasant environment, and will support fairer and safer development that is of higher quality, more efficient and more sustainable.

复合句：一个主句Building an eco-civilization and promoting development will meet demand and will support fairer and safer development，一个从句that is of higher quality, more efficient and more sustainable，跟在被修饰的名词后，进行必要的限定。

主从复合句点拨：非限定性定语从句就是在整个复合句中作定语成分，对前面所修饰的整个主句或者主句中的某个词起到补充说明的作用，用逗号与主句隔开。

构词与常用搭配

structure（*n.*）结构：由struc建设、结构+名词后缀-ture构成。

常用搭配：family structure, social structure

facilitate（v.）促使：由fac-做，作+-ile形容词词尾（e略）+-ity名词词尾（y略）+-ate动词词尾构成。

常用搭配：facilitate access, facilitate learning

coordinate（v.）to make many different things work effectively as a whole协调：由co-共同+-ordin-秩序，顺序+-ate动词词尾构成。

常用搭配：coordinate with, a coordinated approach

feature（v.）以……为特色：由-feat-做，作+-ure名词词尾构成。

常用搭配：distinguishing feature, physical feature

carbon（n.）碳：由carb-碳+-on名词词尾，物质构成。

常用搭配：carbon dioxide, carbon emission, low-carbon

standard（n.）标准：来源于古法语 estendre（伸展）

常用搭配：living standard, academic standard, moral standard

circular（a.）环形的：由-circ-圆+-ular形容词词尾构成。

常用搭配：circular building, circular tour, circular economy

demand（n.）要求：由de-加强意义+-mand-命令构成。

常用搭配：in demand, meet the demand

quality（n.）质量：由qual-性质+-ity名词词尾构成。

常用搭配：high quality, product quality

efficient（a.）效率高的：由ef-出+-fici-做+ent形容词词尾构成。

常用搭配：fuel efficient, efficient method

Crossword Puzzle

Across

4. to include someone or something as an important part
6. to make something possible or easier
8. shaped like a circle
9. a level of quality
10. the way in which the parts of a system or object are arranged or organized, or a system arranged in this way

Down

1. to ask for something forcefully, in a way that shows that you do not expect to be refused
2. a chemical element that is an important part of other substances such as coal and oil, as well as being contained in all plants and animals
3. working or operating quickly and effectively in an organized way
5. how good or bad something is
7. to make many different things work effectively as a whole

The Beautiful China Initiative "美丽中国" 倡议

Chinese government wants to do its bit for the Beautiful China Initiative, and also to sow the seeds of ecological conservation in the entire society, among the Chinese youth in particular. All Chinese people are called on to act as participators and promoters in the endeavor for ecological conservation. With perseverance and accumulated efforts, we will be able to achieve the goal of the initiative, making our country's sky bluer, mountains lusher, waters clearer and the environment more beautiful.

Reading Comprehension

Background Information

中华文明是和谐的，她尊重自然、热爱自然，蕴含着丰富的生态文化。2017年以来，为了要把生态文明融入政治、经济、文化等各方面建设当中去，数封倡议书的通过使建设美丽中国不再是一纸空谈。每位公民尤其是年轻人都要积极成为良好生态环境创建的参与者和推动者。只要我们坚持不懈，有理想、有目标，就一定能实现美丽中国倡议，使祖国的天更蓝、水更美；这不仅仅是环境优美，更是中华文明持续发展的根基和关键。

Critical Thinking

Question One: What can we do to make China beautiful?

Question Two: What challenges might we meet with in the process of carrying out the Beautiful China Initiative?

Question Three: Is there any correlation between the Beautiful China Initiative and the construction of a community with a shared future for mankind?

Language Focus

英语句子结构上具有后开放性特点，因此在使用英语表达时应该先将句子的主干提取出来，最后再添上句子的其他附加成分。

句子主干 指的是构成一个完整句子的框架，主要包括主语、谓语、宾语、表语等基本句子成分。

本语篇一共由3个句子构成，它们的句子主干分别是：

☆Government wants to do its bit and also to sow the seeds.

☆People are called on.

☆We will be able to achieve the goal.

句子附加成分 指的是去除一个完整句子中的主干部分剩余的修饰、补充说明部分，主要包括定语、状语、宾语补足语、主语补足语、同位语、插入语这几个基本句子成分。

本语篇的句子附加成分如下：

★Chinese（形容词作定语）

★Beautiful（形容词作定语）

★China（名词作定语）

★for the initiative（介词短语作状语）

★also（副词作状语）

★of conservation（介词短语作定语）

★ecological（形容词作定语）

★in the society（介词短语作状语）

★entire（形容词作定语）

★among the Chinese youth（介词短语作状语）

★in particular（介词短语作状语）

★as participators and promoters（介词短语作状语）

★in the endeavor for conservation（介词短语作状语）

★with perseverance and efforts（介词短语作状语）

★accumulated（过去分词作定语）

★of the initiative（介词短语作定语）

★our country's（名词所有格作定语）

★making sky blue（现在分词短语作状语）

非谓语动词 是指动词形式有一定的变换，在句子中不作谓语，因此它不受主语的限制。非谓语动词在英语中很常见。它可以在句子中充当主语、宾语、表语、定

113

语、状语、补语等句子成分。非谓语动词有以下三种形式：

◆动词不定式：to do／to be

◆动名词：doing／being

◆分词，一个是现在分词：doing／being；另一个是过去分词：done／been。

本语篇中非谓语动词的使用：

◇**making** our country's sky bluer, mountains lusher, waters clearer and the environment more beautiful 现在分词短语作伴随状语

句子类型 主要包括简单句、复合句和并列句。在用英文表达时，尽量得体、恰当地交叉使用它们。简单句是指，一个主语或者两个以上主语加上一个谓语或者两个以上谓语构成的句子。复合句是指，一个主句加上一个或者多个从句构成的句子。并列句是指，两个以上简单句由并列连词连在一起构成的句子。

本语篇中句子类型的使用：

◎Chinese government wants to do its bit for the Beautiful China initiative, and also to sow the seeds of ecological conservation in the entire society, among the Chinese youth in particular.

简单句：一个主语Chinese government，一个谓语wants又由并列连词and连接的两个并列宾语to do its bit 和 to sow the seeds。

◎All Chinese people are called on to act as participators and promoters in the endeavor for ecological conservation.

简单句：一个主语all Chinese people，一个谓语are called on。

◎With perseverance and accumulated efforts, we will be able to achieve the goal of the initiative, making our country's sky bluer, mountains lusher, waters clearer and the environment more beautiful.

简单句：一个主语we，一个谓语will be able to achieve。

简单句点拨：判断一个句子是否为简单句，需要确定这个句子是否只有一套主谓结构。但是，简单句也可能是含有一套复杂的主谓结构，因为一套主谓结构并不是只能有一个主语、一个谓语。

构词与常用搭配

initiative（*n.*）倡议：由in-向内+-it-行，走+-i-+-ative 形容词词尾构成。

常用搭配：take the initiative，on one's own initiative

bit（*n.*）少量：词源同 bite，咬，指咬下的一小口。

常用搭配：do one's bit，a bit of

sow（*v.*）播种：来自古英语 sawan，播种，播撒

常用搭配：sow the seeds，sow doubt

conservation（*n.*）保护：由con-加强意义+-serv-保持+-ation 名词词尾构成。

常用搭配：energy conservation，environmental conservation

entire（*a.*）整个的：来自拉丁文integrum，整体。

常用搭配：entire life，entire society

participate（*n.*）参与：由part-局部+-i-+-cip-拿+-ate动词词尾构成。

常用搭配：participate in，participating countries

endeavor（*n.*）尝试：由en-进入，使，-deavor，债务，责任构成。

常用搭配：at every endeavor，in the endeavor for

perseverance（*n.*）坚持不懈：动词persevere由per-完全的，-severe严格的，严厉的构成。

常用搭配：with perseverance，full of perseverance

accumulate（*v.*）积累：由ac-来+cumul-堆积+-ate动词词尾构成。

常用搭配：accumulate experiences，an accumulation of

lush（*a.*）郁郁葱葱的：词源同lax，后用来形容植物枝叶嫩的，茂盛的。

常用搭配：lush countryside，a lush apartment

Crossword Puzzle

Across

4. continued effort and determination

7. to take part in or become involved in an activity

8. a small piece or amount of something

9. to put seeds in or on the ground so that plants will grow

10. to collect a large number of things over a long period of time

Down

1. whole or complete, with nothing missing

2. having a lot of green, healthy plants, grass, and trees

3. the protection of plants and animals, natural areas, and interesting and important structures and buildings, especially from the damaging effects of human activity

5. a new plan or process to achieve something or solve a problem

6. an attempt to do something

Energy Conservation and Emissions Reduction 节能减排

One of the biggest challenges we face now is climate change. Energy conservation and emissions reduction becomes the focus for the whole world when it comes to fighting climate change and saving the future of earth. The more energy we produce and consume, the more at risk our planet would be. Therefore, we will strive to improve policies and mechanisms for energy conservation and emission reduction. Conserving energy is the key to the solution. If we reduce the use and subsequently limit production, we can successfully limit harmful carbon emissions at least for now. China will scale up its intended, nationally determined contributions by adopting more vigorous policies and measures.

Reading Comprehension

Background Information

节能减排从广义上讲是指节约物质资源和能量资源，减少废弃物和环境有害物（包括三废和噪声等）排放；狭义上讲，它是指节约能源和减少环境有害物排放。推动能效大幅提升、主要污染物排放总量持续减少，实现节能、减碳，持续改善生态环境质量，为我国实现碳达峰、碳中和目标奠定坚实基础。中国以科学发展观为指导，加快发展现代能源产业，坚持节约资源、保护环境的国策，把建设资源节约型、环境友好型社会放在发展战略的突出位置，增强可持续发展能力，建设创新型国家，为全球经济发展和环境治理作出更大贡献。

Critical Thinking

Question One：Why should we conserve energy? How should people deal with non-renewable resources?

Question Two：How can we reduce emissions? Besides energy saving and emission reduction, what else can human beings do to protect our green environment?

Question Three：Have you ever thought over protecting the Earth? What actions will you take without hesitation?

Language Focus

英语句子结构上具有后开放性特点，因此在使用英语表达时应该先将句子的主干提取出来，最后再添上句子的其他附加成分。

句子主干 指的是构成一个完整句子的框架，主要包括几个基本句子成分：主

语、谓语、宾语、表语。

本语篇一共由7个句子构成，它们的句子主干分别是：

☆One is change.

☆Conservation and reduction becomes the focus.

☆Our planet would be at risk.

☆We will strive.

☆Conserving energy is the key.

☆We can limit emissions.

☆China will scale up contributions.

句子附加成分 指的是去除一个完整句子中的主干部分剩余的修饰、补充说明部分，主要包括几个基本句子成分：定语、状语、宾语补足语、主语补足语、同位语、插入语。

本语篇的句子附加成分如下：

★we face now（定语从句修饰名词challenges）

★when it comes to fighting climate change and saving the future of earth（时间状语从句"当谈到"，to是介词，后面加名词或动名词）

★The more..., the more...（是一个复合句，表示一方的程度随着另一方的变化而变化，其中的两个the都是副词，而不是冠词。前面的句子是状语从句，后面的句子是主句。the用在形容词或副词的比较级前，more代表形容词或副词的比较级。强调宾语energy、表语at risk，把它们提到句首。）

★at risk（介词短语作表语）

★for energy conservation and emission reduction（介词短语作目的状语）

★to the solution（介词短语作定语修饰名词key）

★If we reduce the use and subsequently limit production（if引导的条件状语从句）

★by adopting more vigorous policies and measures（介词短语作方式状语）

非谓语动词 是指动词在句子中不作谓语时的形式，因此它不受主语的限制。非谓语动词在英语句子中使用频繁且广泛。它可以在句子中充当除了谓语之外的其他成分，主语、宾语、表语、定语、状语、补语等。非谓语动词分为3大类：

◆动词不定式：to do/to be

◆动名词：doing/being

◆分词，一个是现在分词：doing/being；另一个是过去分词：done/been。

本语篇中非谓语动词的使用：

◇**fighting** climate change and **saving** the future of earth 动名词短语作介词to的宾语

◇**to improve** policies and mechanisms 动词不定式作strive的宾语

◇**conserving** energy 动名词短语作主语

◇**adopting** more vigorous policies and measures 动名词短语作介词by的宾语

句子类型 主要包括：简单句、复合句和并列句。在用英文表达时，尽量得体、恰当地交叉使用它们。简单句是指，一个主语或者两个、多个并列主语加上一个谓语或者两个、多个并列谓语构成的句子。复合句是指，一个主句加上一个或者多个从句构成的句子。并列句是指，由并列连词把两个或多个简单句连在一起构成的句子。

本语篇中句子类型的使用：

◎One of the biggest challenges we face now is climate change.

复合句：一个主句One of the biggest challenges is climate change，一个定语从句we face now。

◎Energy conservation and emission reduction becomes the focus for the whole world when it comes to fighting climate change and saving the future of earth.

复合句：一个主句Energy conservation and emission reduction becomes the focus for the whole world，一个状语从句when it comes to fighting climate change and saving the future of earth。

◎The more energy we produce and consume, the more at risk our planet would be.

复合句：一个主句the more at risk our planet would be，一个状语从句The more energy we produce and consume。

◎Therefore, we will strive to improve policies and mechanisms for energy conservation and emission reduction.

简单句：一个主语we，一个谓语will strive，宾语to improve policies and mechanisms。

◎Conserving energy is the key to the solution.

119

简单句：一个主语Conserving energy，一个系动词is，一个表语the key。

◎If we reduce the use and subsequently limit production, we can successfully limit harmful carbon emissions at least for now.

复合句：一个主句we can successfully limit harmful carbon emissions at least for now.

一个状语从句：If we reduce the use and subsequently limit production.

◎China will scale up its intended nationally determined contributions by adopting more vigorous policies and measures.

简单句：一个主语China，一个谓语will scale。

主从复合句点拨：无论是主句还是从句，叫作"句"就一定有谓语动词。从句也是句子，判定是什么从句就看该从句在整个复合句中充当什么句子成分。比如，状语从句在句中起状语作用，修饰主句中的谓语动词、形容词或副词。引导状语从句的关联词是某些从属连词，例如when，as，because，as if，where等等。状语从句在句中的位置比较灵活，可置于句首、句末或句中。

构词与常用搭配

conservation（*n.*）保护；节约：由动词conserve（保护；节约）加上名词后缀-ation构成。动词conserve是由表示"保持"的词根serv加上前缀con-=together（一起）演变来的

常用搭配：the conservation of water / fuel，conservation projects，conservation measures，soil and water conservation，conservation law

emission（*n.*）发出；排放：由动词emit（发出）加上名词后缀-ssion构成。动词emit是由表示"送，派"的词根mit加上前缀e-（出）演变来的

常用搭配：the emission of carbon dioxide into the atmosphere，clean up industrial emissions，reducing greenhouse gas emission，air pollutant emission control，vehicle emission

focus（*n.*）焦点；中心点：源自一个表示"火炉"的拉丁语词，后来引申为"集中点"

常用搭配：focus on objects，focus the camera on the children，a focus for debate，out-of-focus photograph，out of focus，auto-focus

consume（*v.*）消耗：动词consume是由表示"拿，取"的词根sume加上前缀con-（共同）演变来的。名词consumer消费者，用户；consumption消费

常用搭配：consume large amounts of fossil fuels，was quickly consumed by fire，consume an unbalanced diet，consume much physical strength，consume a lot of electricity

strive（*v.*）力求；斗争：源自中古英语 striven（艰难尝试，奋斗）

常用搭配：strive against corruption，strive for the victory，strive to reach a higher level，strive for a breakthrough，strive for top performance，strive to meet the needs of

mechanism（*n.*）机械装置，机制；结构：是由表示"机器"的词根mech加上后缀-ism（具备某种性质）构成

常用搭配：a natural defence mechanism，mechanism of price controls，a survival mechanism，a delicate watch mechanism

subsequently（*adv.*）随后，接着：由形容词subsequent（随后的）加上副词后缀-ly构成。形容词subsequent是由表示"跟随"的词根sequ加上前缀sub-（下，后面）

常用搭配：in subsequent years，subsequent events，subsequent actions，be subsequent to，subsequent experience，in subsequent issues of the magazine

harmful（*a.*）有害的：由harm（*n.*，*v.* 伤害；损害）加形容词后缀-ful构成的形容词。反义词harmless（无害的）

常用搭配：be harmful to children's teeth，the harmful effects of alcohol，the harmful substances in，harmful environmental change

intended（*a.*）有意的；预期的：由动词intend（打算，想要）的过去分词演变为形容词。动词intend是由表示"伸展，趋向"的词根 tend构成。

常用搭配：the intended purpose，the intended audience，intended target，be intended for children，intended visit

adopt（*v.*）领养；采用：adopt是由表示"选择choose"的词根opt构成。相同词根构成的单词：adoptable 可采用的，可收养的；option选择；optional 可以任选的，随意的。

常用搭配：to adopt a child，have her baby adopted，adopt different approaches，adopt the new policy，adopt a name/title/language

vigorous（*a.*）有力的；精力充沛的：vigorous是由表示"生命life"的词根vig加上形容词的后缀-ous构成。

常用搭配：a vigorous young man，take vigorous exercise，a strong and vigorous politician，a vigorous market，make a vigorous speech in defence of

measure（n.）措施；度量单位（v.）测量：measure是由表示"计量，测量"的词根meas构成。同根词measurable（可测量的）

常用搭配：take measures，beyond measure，in a measure，measuring equipment / instruments，measure the length and width of，measure six metres in width

Crossword Puzzle

Across

2. attempt by employing effort
7. the preservation and careful management of the environment and of natural resources
8. spend extravagantly
9. the concentration of attention or energy on something

Down

1. choose and follow; as of theories, ideas, policies, strategies or plans
2. happening at a time subsequent to a reference time
3. intentional or planned
4. the technical aspects of doing something
5. a substance that is emitted or released
6. injurious to physical or mental health

Sustainability and Green Development in Guilin 桂林的可持续绿色发展

Guilin, located in the Guangxi Zhuang Autonomous Region, is boosting green growth and prioritizing the preservation of the Lijiang River in its sustainable development plan. Lijiang River is one of China's most famed scenic attractions, where limestone karst hills stand erectly alongside the river. It is expected to build and upgrade the villages along the Lijiang River and transform the tourism distribution center to promote sustainable ecological development of the region. The local government will restore the entire basin and manage projects in landscape, forest, field, lake and grass. Guilin has also advanced the integrated development of urban and rural areas to speed up cultural prosperity and harmony.

Reading Comprehension

Background Information

桂林市是世界著名的风景旅游城市和中国历史文化名城，是广西东北部地区及桂湘交界地区的政治、经济、文化、科技中心。桂林市致力于构建绿色制造体系，发展经济效益高、资源消耗少、高科技、低污染的新型工业模式，构建绿色低碳的现代产业体系，从而实现高质量的产业发展与环境保护齐头并进。

Critical Thinking

Question One: Besides Guilin, should all the cities or even cosmopolises develop its economy in sustainable and environment-friendly way?

Question Two: What will make Guilin unique besides its beautiful scenery? If you are an urban engineer, what engineering solutions will you provide to enhance how people live, work, and play?

Question Three: Will you describe the future of Guilin under its integrated development?

Language Focus

英语句子结构上具有后开放性特点，因此在使用英语表达时应该先将句子的主干提取出来，最后再添上句子的其他附加成分。

句子主干 指的是构成一个完整句子的框架，主要包括几个基本句子成分：主

语、谓语、宾语、表语。

本语篇一共由5个句子构成，它们的句子主干分别是：

☆Guilin is boosting growth and prioritizing the preservation.

☆River is one.

☆It is expected to build and upgrade the villages.

☆The government will restore the basin and manage projects.

☆Guilin has advanced the development.

句子附加成分 指的是去除一个完整句子中的主干部分剩余的修饰、补充说明部分，主要包括几个基本句子成分：定语、状语、宾语补足语、主语补足语、同位语、插入语。

本语篇的句子附加成分如下：

★located in the Guangxi Zhuang Autonomous Region（过去分词短语作插入语，补充说明额外信息：地点）

★sustainable development plan（形容词sustainable和名词development一起作定语）

★most famed（形容词最高级作定语）

★alongside the Lijiang River（介词短语作地点状语）

★It is expected to（it作形式主语，动词不定式是真正主语）

★the tourism distribution center（名词tourism 和distribution作定语修饰center）

★of urban and rural areas（介词短语作后置定语）

★to speed up cultural prosperity and harmony（动词不定式作目的状语）

非谓语动词 是指动词在句子中不作谓语时的形式，因此它不受主语的限制。非谓语动词在英语句子中使用频繁且广泛。它可以在句子中充当除了谓语之外的其他成分，主语、宾语、表语、定语、状语、补语等。非谓语动词分为3大类：

◆动词不定式：to do/to be

◆动名词：doing/being

◆分词，一个是现在分词：doing/being；另一个是过去分词：done/been。

本语篇中非谓语动词的使用：

◇**located** in the Guangxi Zhuang Autonomous Region（过去分词短语，插入语，前后有逗号分开）

◇**to build** and **upgrade** the villages 不定式短语作主语，it是形式主语

◇**to promote** 动词不定式短语作状语表目的

◇the **integrated** development 过去分词作定语

◇**to speed up** cultural prosperity and **harmony** 动词不定式短语作状语表目的

句子类型 主要包括：简单句、复合句和并列句。在用英文表达时，尽量得体、恰当地交叉使用它们。简单句是指，一个主语或者两个、多个并列主语加上一个谓语或者两个、多个并列谓语构成的句子。复合句是指，一个主句加上一个或者多个从句构成的句子。并列句是指，由并列连词把两个或多个简单句连在一起构成的句子。

本语篇中句子类型的使用：

◎Guilin，located in the Guangxi Zhuang Autonomous Region，is boosting green growth and prioritizing the preservation of the Lijiang River in its sustainable development plan.

简单句：一个主语Guilin，两个谓语is boosting，prioritizing。

◎Lijiang River is one of China's most famed scenic attractions，where limestone karst hills stand erectly alongside the river.

复合句：一个主句Lijiang River is one of China's most famed scenic attractions，一个非限制性定语从句 where limestone arst hilld stand erectly alongside the river。

◎It is expected to build and upgrade the villages along the Lijiang River and transform the tourism distribution center to promote sustainable ecological development of the region.

简单句：形式主语it，真正主语是不定式短语to build and upgrade the villages和and transform the center。

◎The local government will restore the entire basin and manage projects in landscape，forest，field，lake and grass.

简单句：一个主语The local government，两个谓语will restore，manage。

◎Guilin has also advanced the integrated development of urban and rural areas to speed up cultural prosperity and harmony.

简单句：一个主语Guilin，一个谓语has also advanced，宾语the integrated development。

主从复合句点拨：无论是主句还是从句，叫作"句"就一定有谓语动词。从句也是句子，判定是什么从句就看该从句在整个复合句中充当什么句子成分。如，定

语从句，尤其是非限定性定语从句在英文表达中使用频率较高，主要起补充说明作用。常用的关系副词有when，where，why等。关系副词where在定语从句中用作地点状语，其先行词须是表地点的名词，或者是有地点含义的抽象名词。

构词与常用搭配

located（a.）坐落的，位于的：动词locate的过去分词。动词locate是由表示"地方，位置"的词根loc加上动词后缀 -ate演变而来。

常用搭配：be located near，be conveniently located within，located within reach

prioritize（v.）按重要性排列；优先处理：由名词priority（先，优先权），加上动词后缀-ize构成。名词priority是由表示"第一，主要的；首要"的词根prior 加上名词后缀-ity演变而来。

常用搭配：prioritize items，prioritize work orders，prioritize tasks

preservation（n.）储藏，保存：由动词preserve（保持；保护）加上名词后缀-tion构成。动词preserve是由表示"保持，留心"的词根serv加上前缀pre-（前，先）演变来的。

常用搭配：building / environmental / food preservation，a preservation group / society，in a state of preservation，preservation of law and order

sustainable（a.）可持续的：由动词sustain（维持；支撑）加上形容词后缀-able构成。动词sustain是由表示"持，握"的词根tain加上前缀sus-（下面）演变来的。

常用搭配：environmentally sustainable，sustainable recovery，sustainable development

famed（a.）著名的：由名词fame（名声，名誉）加上形容词后缀-ed构成。名词fame是由表示"名声，名誉"的词根fam构成。

常用搭配：a famed poet and musician，be famed both at home and abroad，be famed for

attraction（n.）吸引力：由动词attract（吸引）加上名词后缀-tion构成。动词attract是由表示"拉，引"的词根tract加上前缀at-（朝，向）演变来的。

常用搭配：a tourist attraction，attractions of，hold little attraction for，gravitational / magnetic attraction

upgrade（v.）提升；升级：upgrade是由表示"步，级"的词根grad加上前缀up-

（向上）构成。

常用搭配：on the upgrade，upgrade facilities，upgrade service standard，upgrade systems，upgrade computer

transform（*v.*）使改变形态：transform是由表示"形"的词根form加上前缀trans-（转变，转换）构成。

常用搭配：transform the environment，transform the mountains by afforestation，transform the logical thoughts into practical actions，transform electricity energy to kinetic energy

distribution（*n.*）分配，分布：由动词distribute（分配，分发）加上名词后缀-ion构成。动词distribute是由表示"交给"的词根tribut加上前缀dis-（分离，分开）演变而来的。

常用搭配：worldwide distribution systems，distribution costs，unfair distribution of wealth，geographical distribution of the disease

ecological（*a.*）生态的，生态学的：由名词ecology（生态学）加上形容词后缀-ical构成。名词ecology是由表示"生态"的词根eco加上后缀-logy（学说）构成。

常用搭配：an ecological disaster，ecological movement，ecological balance，ecological protection，ecological compensation，ecological construction

restore（*v.*）恢复；归还：restore是由表示"储藏，存放"的动词store加上前缀re-（再，重新）构成，引申词义恢复，修复。

常用搭配：restore public confidence，restore faith，restore to health，restore traditions

integrated（*a.*）完整的；整体的：由动词integrate（合并；成为一体）的过去分词演变成形容词。动词integrate是由表示"完整"的词根integr加上后缀-ate（使……）构成。

常用搭配：an integrated transport system，integrated circuits，integrated into the community，integrated cultivation，live in a fully integrated，supportive society

prosperity（*n.*）繁荣，兴旺：prosperity由表示"前"的前缀pro- 和表示"希望"的词根sper及名词后缀-ity构成。形容词prosperous "兴旺的，繁荣的"。

常用搭配：future prosperity，peace and prosperity，economic prosperity，attain prosperity，a scene of prosperity

harmony（*n.*）和谐，融洽：来源于希腊神话中代表和谐和协调的女神 Harmonia 的名字。同源词：harmonic，harmonious

常用搭配：harmony of colour，social / racial harmony，in harmony with，singing in harmony，regional harmony and stability

Crossword Puzzle

Across

2. to improve, especially something that was old or outdated

7. formed or united into a whole

8. the activity of protecting something from loss or danger

9. compatibility in opinion and action

10. the quality of arousing interest; being attractive or something that attracts

11. characterized by the interdependence of living organisms in an environment

Down

1. capable of being sustained

3. the spatial property of being scattered about over an area or volume

4. situated in a particular spot or position

5. an economic state of growth with rising profits and full employment

6. change or alter in form, appearance, or nature

8. assign a priority to

Internet of Vehicles in China 中国"车联网"

The Internet of vehicles in China is practicing the transformation and sustainable development of green and low-carbon. The Chinese IoV aims for green, low-carbon and environmental-friendly infrastructure construction, which utilizes renewable energy and creates an intelligent and digital transport system. Green travel is advocated widely in China.

Reading Comprehension

Background Information

车联网的英文Internet of Vehicles经常缩写为IoV，车联网指以下三种情况：一是车辆之间的网络互通互联，二是车辆内部的网络连接，三是车辆在行驶中的移动网络连接。中国的车联网起步于2009年。中国上汽通用汽车有限公司率先开启了车联网应用的实质性探索。2018—2020年，中国车联网行业用户规模均逐年上升。车联网行业渗透率已达48.8%，超过全球车联网行业渗透率，车联网用户规模达到约为14000万辆。预计到2025年中国车联网行业渗透率将超过75%，用户规模将超过3.8亿辆。

Critical Thinking

Question One: How will the Internet of vehicles promote the Green, Low-Carbon and Circular Development in China?

Question Two: How much do you know about smart transportation? What are you willing to do for it?

Language Focus

英语句子结构上具有后开放性特点，因此在使用英语表达时应该先将句子的主干提取出来，最后再添上句子的其他附加成分。

句子主干 指的是构成一个完整句子的框架，主要包括几个基本句子成分：主语、谓语、宾语、表语。

本语篇一共由3个句子构成，它们的句子主干分别是：

☆The Internet is practicing the transformation and developmet.

☆The IoV aims for construction.

☆Travel is advocated.

句子附加成分 指的是去除一个完整句子中的主干部分剩余的修饰、补充说明部分，主要包括几个基本句子成分：定语、状语、宾语补足语、主语补足语、同位语、插入语。

本语篇的句子附加成分如下：

★ of vehicles（介词短语作后置定语）

★ in China（介词短语作后置定语）

★ sustainable（形容词作定语）

★ of green and low-carbon（介词短语作后置定语）

★ Chinese（形容词作定语）

★ green，low-carbon and environmental-friendly（3个形容词并列作定语）

★ infrastructure（名词作定语）

★ which utilizes renewable energy and creates an intelligent and digital transport system（非限定性定语从句）

★ Green（形容词作定语）

★ widely（副词作状语）

★ in China（介词短语作地点状语）

非谓语动词 是指动词在句子中不作谓语时的形式，因此它不受主语的限制。非谓语动词在英语句子中使用频繁且广泛。它可以在句子中充当除了谓语之外的其他成分：主语、宾语、表语、定语、状语、补语等。非谓语动词分为3大类：

◆ 动词不定式：to do / to be

◆ 动名词：doing / being

◆ 分词，一个是现在分词：doing / being；另一个是过去分词：done / been。

本语篇中未见到非谓语动词的使用。

句子类型 主要包括：简单句、复合句和并列句。在用英文表达时，尽量得体、恰当地交叉使用它们。简单句是指，一个主语或者两个、多个并列主语加上一个谓语或者两个、多个并列谓语构成的句子。复合句是指，一个主句加上一个或者多个从句构成的句子。并列句是指，由并列连词把两个或多个简单句连在一起构成的句子。

本语篇中句子类型的使用：

◎ The Internet of vehicles in China is practicing the transformation and sustainable development of green and low-carbon.

简单句：一个主语Internet，一个谓语is practicing。

◎The Chinese IoV aims for green, low-carbon and environmental-friendly infrastructure construction, which utilizes renewable energy and creates an intelligent and digital transport system.

复合句：一个主句The Chinese IoV aims for green, low-carbon and environmental-friendly infrastructure construction, 一个从句which utilizes renewable energy and creates an intelligent and digital transport system。

◎Green travel is advocated widely in China.

简单句：一个主语travel, 一个谓语is advocated。

主从复合句点拨：无论是主句还是从句，叫作"句"就一定有谓语动词。从句也是句子，判定是什么从句就看该从句在整个复合句中充当什么句子成分。如，定语从句就是该从句在整个复合句中作定语成分。定语从句，尤其是非限定性定语从句在英文表达中使用频率较高。

构词与常用搭配

vehicle（*n.*）车辆：由词根vey=way（道路）加上名词后缀-icle（工具）构成，引申为"交通工具"。

常用搭配：electric vehicle, underwater vehicle, heavy vehicle, utility vehicle, military vehicle, drive vehicle, use vehicle, buy vehicle

transformation（*n.*）转变：由词根form（形状）加上前缀trans-（改变），再加上名词后缀-tion构成。

常用搭配：a complete transformation, transformation projects, transformation in / of

sustainable（*a.*）可持续的：由词根tain（握）加前缀sus-（接着），再加上形容词后缀-able构成。

常用搭配：sustainable development, sustainable recovery, sustainable resource, sustainable revival, sustainable agriculture, sustainable forest

infrastructure（*n.*）基础设施：由词根structure（结构）加上前缀infra-（在下方）构成，引申为"基础建设；基础设施"。

常用搭配：infrastructure projects, IT infrastructure, infrastructural development, infrastructure construction, city infrastructure, road infrastructure

utilize（*v.*）利用；使用：由词根uti=use（用）加上动词后缀-ize构成。

常用搭配：utilize efficiently，utilize resources，utilize technology

advocate（*v.*）倡导：由词根voc=call（喊）加上前缀ad-表示"加强"，再加上动词后缀-ate构成，加强说，喊，即为"支持呼吁"，引申为"倡导"。

常用搭配：advocate for，an advocate of，advocate use，advocate policy

Crossword Puzzle

Across

5. the basic systems and services that are necessary for a country or an organization to run smoothly

7. involving the use of natural products and energy in a way that does not harm the environment

Down

1. to support something publicly

2. a qualitative or complete change in somebody or something

3. put into service；make work or employ something for a particular purpose or for its natural purpose

4. Actively working in，engaging in，or observing something，especially a particular profession or religion

6. a thing that is used for transporting people or goods from one place to another

Building a Green Nation 建设绿色国家

China must adhere to the concept that lucid waters and lush mountains are valuable assets. The government highlights the nation's efforts to promote ecological advancement, increase afforestation and improve people's living environment. China should scientifically promote afforestation nationwide and raise the quantity and quality of forest and grassland resources in order to increase carbon sinks. However, it's a long-term task to conserve and restore the fundamental improvement of the environment, which requires arduous efforts. As forests and grasslands are of fundamental and strategic significance to the country's ecological security, China has entered a key period in improving its environment.

Reading Comprehension

Background Information

"我们既要绿水青山，也要金山银山。"生动地表达了中国推进生态文明建设的鲜明态度和坚定决心。实现保护生态环境与经济发展的均衡协调发展是我们社会经济发展的努力目标。生态文明建设必须坚持在发展中保护、在保护中发展，实现和谐共进。只有坚持绿色发展和节能环保，推进生态文明建设，才能构建美丽中国，形成绿色发展新格局。

Critical Thinking

Question One: Why should we promote ecological advancement? Can the balance be achieved between rapid development of science and technology and protection of ecology?

Question Two: Will you describe an ideal picture of green nation?

Question Three: What can ordinary people do for building a green nation? Have you ever planted any trees? Do you support green and low-carbon traveling?

Language Focus

英语句子结构上具有后开放性特点，因此在使用英语表达时应该先将句子的主干提取出来，最后再添上句子的其他附加成分。

句子主干 指的是构成一个完整句子的框架，主要包括几个基本句子成分：主语、谓语、宾语、表语。

本语篇一共由5个句子构成，它们的句子主干分别是：

☆China must adhere to the concept.

☆The government highlights the efforts.

☆China should promote afforestation and raise the quantity and quality.

☆It's a task.

☆China has entered a period.

句子附加成分 指的是去除一个完整句子中的主干部分剩余的修饰、补充说明部分，主要包括几个基本句子成分：定语、状语、宾语补足语、主语补足语、同位语、插入语。

本语篇的句子附加成分如下：

★lucid waters and lush mountains（并列名词短语作定语从句的主语）

★ecological advancement（ecological是形容词作定语）

★people's living environment（people's是名词所有格作定语）

★of forest and grassland resources（介词短语作后置定语）

★carbon sinks（carbon是名词作定语。carbon sinks：碳汇，是指通过植树造林、植被恢复等措施，吸收大气中的二氧化碳，从而减少温室气体在大气中浓度的过程、活动或机制。）

★a long-term task（形容词long-term作定语）

★of fundamental and strategic significance（介词短语作表语）

★a key period（key是名词作定语）

★in improving its environment（介词短语作定语）

非谓语动词 是指动词在句子中不作谓语时的形式，因此它不受主语的限制。非谓语动词在英语句子中使用频繁且广泛。它可以在句子中充当除了谓语之外的其他成分，主语、宾语、表语、定语、状语、补语等。非谓语动词分为3大类：

◆动词不定式：to do / to be

◆动名词：doing / being

◆分词，一个是现在分词：doing / being；另一个是过去分词：done / been。

本语篇中非谓语动词的使用：

◇to **promote** ecological advancement, **increase** afforestation and **improve** people's living environment 动词不定式短语作状语表目的

◇in order **to increase** carbon sinks 动词不定式短语作状语表目的

◇**to conserve** and **restore** the fundamental improvement of the environment 动词不定式短语作主语，it是形式主语

◇in **improving** its environment 动名词短词作介词in的宾语

句子类型 主要包括：简单句、复合句和并列句。在用英文表达时，尽量得体、恰当地交叉使用它们。简单句是指，一个主语或者两个、多个并列主语加上一个谓语或者两个、多个并列谓语构成的句子。复合句是指，一个主句加上一个或者多个从句构成的句子。并列句是指，由并列连词把两个或多个简单句连在一起构成的句子。

本语篇中句子类型的使用：

◎China must adhere to the concept that lucid waters and lush mountains are valuable assets.

复合句：一个主句China must adhere to the concept；一个从句that lucid waters and lush mountains are valuable assets。

◎The government highlights the nation's efforts to promote ecological advancement, increase afforestation and improve people's living environment.

简单句：一个主语The government，一个谓语highlights。

◎China should scientifically promote afforestation nationwide and raise the quantity and quality of forest and grassland resources in order to increase carbon sinks.

简单句：一个主语China，两个谓语promote和raise。

◎However, it's a long-term task to conserve and restore the fundamental improvement of the environment, which requires arduous efforts.

复合句：一个主句it's a long-term task to conserve and restore the fundamental improvement of the environment；一个从句which requires arduous efforts。

◎As forests and grasslands are of fundamental and strategic significance to the country's ecological security, China has entered a key period in improving its environment.

复合句：一个主句China has entered a key period in improving its environment；

一个从句As forests and grasslands are of fundamental and strategic significance to the country's ecological security。

主从复合句点拨：无论是主句还是从句，叫作"句"就一定有谓语动词。从句也是句子，判定是什么从句就看该从句在整个复合句中充当什么句子成分。如，定语从句就是该从句在整个复合句中作定语成分。引导定语从句的关联词为关系代词和关系副词。关系代词在定语从句中可用作主语、宾语、定语等；关系副词在定语从句中只用作状语。

构词与常用搭配

adhere（v.）遵守；附着：由前缀ad-（去，往）加上词根here（粘住）构成动词。

常用搭配：adhere to a strict diet，adhere to a strict practice，adhere to principles，adhere to agreement

concept（n.）概念；观念：由前缀con-（共同）加上词根cept（抓住，理解）构成名词。

常用搭配：the basic concepts of，legal concepts，concept of right and wrong

valuable（a.）有价值的；宝贵的：由名词value（价值（观）；重要性）加上形容词后缀-able构成。名词value由表示"价值"的词根val构成。

常用搭配：a valuable experience，valuable information on，valuable antiques，a valuable collection，obtain valuable information

asset（n.）资产：由词根set（足够）加上前缀as-=ad（去）构成。

常用搭配：asset sales / management，financial / capital assets，the net asset value，have assets of，be a great asset to

promote（v.）促进；促销：由前缀pro-（向前）加上词根mot（移动）构成动词。同词根的还有：motion，move。

常用搭配：to promote economic growth，to promote awareness，promote the business of，promote cooperation between，promote products

environment（*n.*）环境：由前缀en-（入，向内）加上词根viron（围，绕）和名词后缀-ment构成。

常用搭配：working / learning environment，political environment，to protect the environment，damage to the environment，a safe environment for

afforestation（*n.*）植树造林：由前缀 af-（同ad-，去，往）加上词根forest（森林）构成名词。反义词 deforest。

常用搭配： afforestation rate，a massive afforestation program，transform the mountains by afforestation，the afforestation of，seeding afforestation project

resource（*n.*）资源，财力：由前缀 re-（再，重复）加上词根source（源泉）构成名词。

常用搭配：natural resources，pool resources，financial resources，resource materials，important strategic resource，the red tourism resource

fundamental（*a.*）基本的；十分重大的：由名词fundament（基础，基本原理）加上形容词后缀-al构成。名词fundament由表示"基础"的词根fund加上名词后缀-ment构成。

常用搭配：pose a fundamental threat to，address fundamental weaknesses，fundamental importance，share fundamental interests

strategic（*a.*）有战略意义的；至关重要的：来自希腊语strategia（军事指挥部）

常用搭配：a strategic decision，new strategic thinking，strategic nuclear weapons，strategic approach，tactical and strategic advantages，strategic thinking skills

security（*n.*）安保措施；债券：由形容词secure（安全的）加上名词后缀-ity构成。形容词secure是由表示"关心"的词根cur加上前缀se-（分离）演变来的。

常用搭配：national security，security checks，security forces / services，security of，strict security measures，government securities and bonds，security guard

Crossword Puzzle

Across

2. serving as an essential component

4. the state of being free from danger or injury

5. the totality of surrounding conditions

8. characterized by toilsome effort to the point of exhaustion; especially physical effort

10. having great material or monetary value especially for use or exchange

11. an abstract or general idea inferred or derived from specific instances

Down

1. a useful or valuable quality

3. the conversion of bare or cultivated land into forest

4. relating to or concerned with strategy

6. follow through or carry out a plan without deviation

7. contribute to the progress or growth of

9. available source of wealth; a new or reserve supply that can be drawn upon when needed

China's Green Development with Recognition and New Opportunities
中国绿色发展：得到认同、迎来新机遇

The world has been impressed by China's blistering economic growth. Now we are expected to gain inspiring experience from its accelerating green transformation through coordinating the economy with the natural environment. It was not the first time that China was awarded the environmental honor for making remarkable contributions to a positive effect on the environment.

Reading Comprehension

Background Information

绿色转型是发展方式的革命性变革，指经济发展转向资源节约、排放减少的绿色发展方式。在人类的发展过程中，科技水平不断进步，物质需求也随之上涨。为保证经济的持续发展，多年来，人们采用高投入、高消费、高污染的发展方式，这使得我们赖以生存的地球以肉眼可见的速度恶化。为此，出现绿色转型发展的要求，即以生态文明建设为主导作用，推动循环经济建设，形成资源节约、减排的绿色发展模式。绿色发展的新理念将加快中国生态文明建设，实现经济可持续发展。中国的绿色转型更注重实际，更强调效率而不是宣传。

Critical Thinking

Question One: What achievements has China made in green development?

Question Two: What opportunities will China meet with in the future green development?

Question Three: What do you think of Chinese solution to environment protection for all mankind?

Language Focus

英语句子结构上具有后开放性特点，因此在使用英语表达时应该先将句子的主干提取出来，最后再添上句子的其他附加成分。

句子主干 指的是构成一个完整句子的框架，主要包括主语、谓语、宾语、表语等基本句子成分。

本语篇一共由3个句子构成，它们的句子主干分别是：

☆ The world has been impressed.

☆We are expected to learn.

☆It was not the time.

句子附加成分 指的是去除一个完整句子中的主干部分剩余的修饰、补充说明部分，主要包括定语、状语、宾语补足语、主语补足语、同位语、插入语这几个基本句子成分。

本语篇的句子附加成分如下：

★China's（名词所有格作定语）

★blistering（现在分词作定语）

★economic（形容词作定语）

★inspiring（现在分词作定语）

★from its transformation（介词短语作状语）

★accelerating（现在分词作定语）

★green（形容词作定语）

★through coordinating the economy and the environment（介词短语作方式状语）

★natural（形容词作定语）

★environmental（形容词作定语）

★remarkable（形容词作定语）

★with respect to an effect（介词短语作状语）

★positive（形容词作定语）

★on the environment（介词短语作定语）

非谓语动词 是指动词形式有一定的变换，在句子中不作谓语，因此它不受主语的限制。非谓语动词在英语中很常见。它可以在句子中充当主语、宾语、表语、定语、状语、补语等句子成分。非谓语动词有以下三种形式：

◆动词不定式：to do / to be

◆动名词：doing / being

◆分词，一个是现在分词：doing / being；另一个是过去分词：done / been。

本语篇中非谓语动词的使用：

◇**blistering** economic growth，**inspiring** lessons和**accelerating** green transformation 现在分词作定语，表示主动、进行

句子类型 主要包括简单句、复合句和并列句。在用英文表达时，尽量得体、恰当地交叉使用它们。简单句是指，一个主语或者两个以上主语加上一个谓语或者两个以上谓语构成的句子。复合句是指，一个主句加上一个或者多个从句构成的句子。并列句是指，两个以上简单句由并列连词连在一起构成的句子。

本语篇中句子类型的使用：

◎The world has been impressed by China's blistering economic growth.

简单句：一个主语The world，一个谓语has been impressed。

◎Now we are expected to learn inspiring lessons from its accelerating green transformation by coordinating the economy and the natural environment.

简单句：一个主语we，一个谓语are expected to learn。

◎It was not the first time that China was awarded the UN's highest environmental prize for remarkable contributions in terms of a positive transformative effect on the environment.

复合句：一个主句It was not the first time，一个从句 that China was awarded。

主语从句点拨：从句作主语就是主语从句。但主语从句通常用形式主语it代替，真正的主语从句放到句子最后，起到平衡整个句子的作用。

构词与常用搭配

recognition（*n.*）承认：由re-再+co-一起+-gn-知道+-ition 名词词尾构成。

常用搭配：in recognition of，beyond recognition，gain recognition for

opportunity（*n.*）机遇：由op-来，临近+-port-运输，携带+un+-ity名词词尾构成。

常用搭配：at every opportunity，a window of opportunity，job opportunity

blistering（*a.*）极快的：blister词源同 ball，指"鼓起来的"。

常用搭配：blistering heat，blistering attack，blistering speed

expect（*v.*）预计：由ex-出，向外（x发音为ks）+-spect看构成。

常用搭配：be expected to，as expected

accelerate（*v.*）加快：由ac-加强意义+-celer-快，速+-ate动词词尾构成。

常用搭配：accelerating rate，accelerate this process

transformation（*n.*）转变：由trans-转变，转换+-form-形+tion名词词尾构成。

常用搭配：dramatic transformation，undergo transformation

award（*v.*）给予：由a-临近+ward看管，看护构成。

常用搭配：award a medal，award pay increases

remarkable（*a.*）非凡的：由re-再+mark 记号+-able形容词词尾构成。

常用搭配：remarkable achievement，remarkable courage，remarkable changes

contribution（*n.*）贡献：由con-加强意义+-tribut-交给+-ion名词词尾构成。

常用搭配：make a contribution，a substantial contribution

positive（*a.*）积极的：由posit-放置+-ive形容词词尾构成。

常用搭配：positive attitude，on the positive side，positive effects

Crossword Puzzle

Across

2. to happen or make something happen sooner or faster

5. an occasion or situation that makes it possible to do something that you want to do or have to do, or the possibility of doing something

6. extremely fast

7. a complete change in the appearance or character of something or someone, especially so that that thing or person is improved

9. agreement that something is true or legal

10. unusual or special and therefore surprising and worth mentioning

Down

1. to give money or a prize following an official decision

3. something that you contribute or do to help produce or achieve something together with other people, or to help make something successful

4. to think or believe something will happen, or someone will arrive

8. full of hope and confidence, or giving cause for hope and confidence

Green Infrastructure Boosted 推动绿色基础设施建设

In order to uphold the country's green development, China will advance the construction of urban environmental infrastructure. The modern environmental infrastructure, a comprehensive, efficient and intelligent system, will have been established in a decade. Sewage disposal capacity will increase dramatically and the handling capacity of household garbage will approach an optimistic figure.

Reading Comprehension

Background Information

绿色基础设施是一个绿色网络系统，包括绿道、湿地、森林、植被等。这种"绿色基础设施"不仅可以节约城市管理成本，而且还可以改善水的质量、减少洪水，还可以应对气候变化对城市产生的影响。绿色基础设施是一个相对于灰色基础设施和社会基础设施的新概念，首先由美国保护基金会和农业部林业局提出。它是一个多元化、多维、互联的网络系统，具有连接性、多功能性等特点。绿色基础设施建成后，将有效减少对灰色基础设施的依赖，降低对自然灾害的敏感性，成为人类赖以生存的重要基础设施。

Critical Thinking

Question One: What can the whole world benefit from the green infrastructure? Do you believe Chinese building green infrastructure will contribute to the ultimate Earth protection? Why or why not?

Question Two: What principles should be followed during the establishment of the green infrastructure?

Language Focus

英语句子结构上具有后开放性特点，因此在使用英语表达时应该先将句子的主干提取出来，最后再添上句子的其他附加成分。

句子主干 指的是构成一个完整句子的框架，主要包括主语、谓语、宾语、表语等基本句子成分。

本语篇一共由3个句子构成，它们的句子主干分别是：

☆China will advance the construction.

☆The infrastructure will have been established.

☆Capacity will increase and capacity will approach a figure.

句子附加成分 指的是去除一个完整句子中的主干部分剩余的修饰、补充说明部分，主要包括定语、状语、宾语补足语、主语补足语、同位语、插入语这几个基本句子成分。

本语篇的句子附加成分如下：

★ the country's（名词所有格作定语）

★ green（形容词作定语）

★ of...infrastructure（介词短语作后置定语）

★ urban（形容词作定语）

★ environmental（形容词作定语）

★ comprehensive（形容词作定语）

★ efficient（形容词作定语）

★ intelligent（形容词作定语）

★ modern（形容词作定语）

★ in a decade（介词短语作时间状语）

★ sewage（名词作定语）

★ disposal（名词作定语）

★ dramatically（副词作状语）

★ handling（现在分词作定语）

★ of household garbage（介词短语作定语）

★ optimistic（形容词作定语）

非谓语动词 是指动词形式有一定的变换，在句子中不作谓语，因此它不受主语的限制。非谓语动词在英语中很常见。它可以在句子中充当主语、宾语、表语、定语、状语、补语等句子成分。非谓语动词有以下三种形式：

◆ 动词不定式：to do／to be

◆ 动名词：doing／being

◆ 分词，一个是现在分词：doing／being；另一个是过去分词：done／been。

本语篇中非谓语动词的使用：

◇ in order **to uphold** the country's green development 不定式作状语，表示目的。

◇ the **handling** capacity 现在分词作定语，表示主动、进行。

句子类型 主要包括简单句、复合句和并列句。在用英文表达时，尽量得体、恰当地交叉使用它们。简单句是指，一个主语或者两个以上主语加上一个谓语或者两个以上谓语构成的句子。复合句是指，一个主句加上一个或者多个从句构成的句子。并列句是指，两个以上简单句由并列连词连在一起构成的句子。

本语篇中句子类型的使用：

◎In order to uphold the country's green development, China will advance the construction of urban environmental infrastructure.

简单句：一个主语China，一个谓语 will advance。

◎The modern environmental infrastructure, a comprehensive, efficient and intelligent system, will have been established in a decade.

简单句：一个主语infrastructure，一个谓语will have been established。

◎Sewage disposal capacity will increase dramatically and the handling capacity of household garbage will approach an optimistic figure.

并列句：由并列连词and连接两个并列分句：第一个分句Sewage disposal capacity will increase dramatically；第二个分句the handling capacity of household garbage will approach an optimistic figure。

简单句、并列句点拨：英文的简单句与并列句的共同特征是，只有并列、顺承、转折等"同等地位"的关系，不存在从属、主次关系。

构词与常用搭配

boost（v.）推动：来自拟声词，同boom。

常用搭配：boost profits, boost confidence, boost sales

advance（v.）促进：来自拉丁语abante，前缀ab，从，从……离开，词根ante前面的。

常用搭配：in advance, advanced technology

infrastructure（n.）基础设施：由infra-下，在下+-struct-建设，结构+-ure构成。

常用搭配：infrastructure development, city infrastructure,

comprehensive（a.）全面的：由com-全部+-prehens-抓住+-ive 形容词词尾构成。

常用搭配：comprehensive study, comprehensive approach, comprehensive school

efficient（a.）效率高的：由ef-出+-fic-做+-i-+-ent形容词词尾构成。

常用搭配：fuel efficient cars, efficient method, efficient use of energy

intelligent（a.）有才智的：由intel-之间，中间+-lig-诵读+-ent形容词词尾构成。

常用搭配：intelligent machine, intelligent life, intelligent system

establish（*v.*）建立：由e-向上+-st-站立+-able（e略）+-ish动词词尾构成。

常用搭配：establish yourself，be established in

sewage（*n.*）污水：由sew，排污，排水+-age，名词后缀构成。

常用搭配：sewage disposal，raw sewage

disposal（*n.*）处理：由dis-分离，分开+-pos-放置+-al构成。

常用搭配：at sb's disposal，waste disposal

capacity（*n.*）容量：由cap-拿+-acity名词词尾构成。

常用搭配：at full capacity，parking capacity，production capacity

Crossword Puzzle

Across

2. to improve or increase something
5. the total amount that can be contained or produced, or（especially of a person or organization）the ability to do a particular thing
6. the basic systems and services, such as transport and power supplies, that a country or organization uses in order to work effectively
7. to go or move something forward, or to develop or improve something
8. working or operating quickly and effectively in an organized way
9. waste matter such as water or human urine or solid waste

Down

1. showing intelligence, or able to learn and understand things easily
3. to start a company or organization that will continue for a long time
4. the act of getting rid of something, especially by throwing it away
5. complete and including everything that is necessary

Section B　Module Project：Global Issues Discussion

　　在国家做出2030年前二氧化碳排放达到峰值、2060年前争取二氧化碳排放中和的庄严承诺，设定"30·60"目标即"双碳"目标后，并发出："目标实现需要社会各界的持续共同努力"的呼吁下，作为懂外语的中国人，你是否准备好了向世界积极传播在实现"双碳"目标过程中，体现中国智慧和中国力量小而美的事迹，从而构成国际传播矩阵贡献自己一分力量？

　　Short Video Project：What endeavors made for the Green, Low-Carbon and Circular Development by Chinese people will you tell the whole world? Could you make them short videos and then post these videos on websites to communicate Chinese solutions to and actions on green development internationally?

Section C　Learners' Presentation

　　目前我国国际传播主张：国内外网民、海外华侨华人、国外记者、国际技术交流人才是当代传播好中国声音的有生力量。除了官方主流媒体平台Facebook和Twitter以外，民营的社交媒体平台Tiktok是一个提升国际传播效能的好例子。为进一步提升我国全面、立体式向世界宣介中国方案、中国智慧的传播效能，我们应积极参与全民外交，借力海外社交平台（例如，YouTube, Instagram照片墙、Snapchat色拉布、Tumblr汤博乐、Pinterest拼趣、Flickr雅虎网络相册）通过他者讲述中国故事，让他国老百姓以自己的亲身经历传播立体真实的中国形象。

Section D   Reflective Assessment

成长档案袋

	Y	N	Achievements
Am I satisfied with my project products?			
Shall I further improve my project products?			
Are my project products popular online?			
Can I communicate Chinese solutions to and actions on green low carbon development internationally?			
Have I mastered the vocabulary, sentence patterns and some background information on green, low-carbon development in China?			

Module Four

What Changes in China Have You Seen?

中国发生了哪些变化？

　　《*春天里*》画面充分表现花卉的正面、侧面、俯仰、横斜的参差变化，山坡的一角花开满山坡的蓝紫色鸢尾花具有多元化和包容性。"山"是中国文化中重要的文学意象和文化母题，透过特定角度把内在与象征的东西展示给观众。（艺术评论家王健）

　　The painting fully demonstrates the varied changes of the blooming blue-purple iris flowers on the hillside from the front, side, high, low and horizontal slope angles, meaning diversity and inclusiveness. "Mountain" is an important literary imagery and motif in Chinese culture, showing the inner and symbolic things to audiences from a certain perspective. (Art critic: WANG Jian)

Section A   Interpretive Input

Profound Changes in Shenzhen深圳巨变

With a longer history than most of the other streets in Shenzhen, Lao Jie (Old Street) has existed for decades. Having the smell of countryside and nature, it was the only road there nearly half a century ago, which was a dirt lane and merged into its surrounding open fields. Having sped up since the 1980s, the change in China's urban landscape has been happening at an ever-increasing rate on an unprecedented scale. In no time at all, the rural villages that once dotted the landscape had simply disappeared.

Reading Comprehension

Background Information

从南海破旧的小渔村，到如今漂亮的国际化大都市，"深圳速度"令世人瞩目；从蛇口"开山第一炮"到如今每平方公里的约8家高新技术企业，再到约三分之二的世界500强被吸引到深圳落户，它已成为中国乃至世界的科技之都。40余载披荆斩棘，深圳人敢干敢闯敢试、敢为人先，创造了一个又一个跨越式发展的奇迹。深圳的崛起无疑是中国改革开放事业的生动写照，深圳的巨大变化成就充分证明：改革开放是决定当代中国命运的关键一步，中国特色社会主义道路能够走得通，更能走得快、走得远、走得好。

Critical Thinking

Question One: What are the contributing factors of tremendous changes of rural areas in China?

Question Two: Where do you prefer to live in, a world-class modernized metropolis or a village with the smell of countryside and nature?

Language Focus

英语句子结构上具有后开放性特点，因此在使用英语表达时应该先将句子的主干提取出来，最后再添上句子的其他附加成分。

句子主干 指的是构成一个完整句子的框架，主要包括几个基本句子成分：主语、谓语、宾语、表语。

本语篇一共由4个句子构成，它们的句子主干分别是：

☆ Lao Jie has existed.

☆ It was the road.

☆ The change has been happening.

☆ The villages had disappeared.

句子附加成分 指的是去除一个完整句子中的主干部分剩余的修饰、补充说明部分，主要包括几个基本句子成分：定语、状语、宾语补足语、主语补足语、同位语、插入语。

本语篇的句子附加成分如下：

★ With a longer history than most of the other streets in Shenzhen（介词短语作原因状语）

★ for decades（介词短语作时间状语）

★ Having the smell of countryside and nature（现在分词短语作伴随状语）

★ only（形容词作状语）

★ there（指示代词作状语）

★ nearly（副词作状语）

★ half a century ago（名词短语作时间状语）

★ which was a dirt lane and merged into its surrounding open fields（非限定性定语从句）

★ Having sped up since the 1980s（现在分词短语作原因状语）

★ in China's urban landscape（介词短语作后置定语）

★ at an ever-increasing rate（介词短语作状语）

★ on an unprecedented scale（介词短语作状语）

★ In no time at all（介词短语作状语）

★ rural（形容词作定语）

★ that once dotted the landscape（限定性定语从句）

★ simply（副词作状语）

非谓语动词 是指动词在句子中不作谓语时的形式，因此它不受主语的限制。非谓语动词在英语句子中使用频繁且广泛。它可以在句子中充当除了谓语之外的其他

成分，主语、宾语、表语、定语、状语、补语等。非谓语动词分为3大类：

◆动词不定式：to do / to be

◆动名词：doing / being

◆分词，一个是现在分词：doing / being；另一个是过去分词：done / been。

本语篇中非谓语动词的使用：

◇**Having** the smell of countryside and nature 现在分词短语作状语表进行、原因

◇**Having** sped up since the 1980s 现在分词短语作状语表进行、原因

句子类型 主要包括：简单句、复合句和并列句。在用英文表达时，尽量得体、恰当地交叉使用它们。简单句是指，一个主语或者两个、多个并列主语加上一个谓语或者两个、多个并列谓语构成的句子。复合句是指，一个主句加上一个或者多个从句构成的句子。并列句是指，由并列连词把两个或多个简单句连在一起构成的句子。

本语篇中句子类型的使用：

◎With a longer history than most of the other streets in Shenzhen, Lao Jie（Old Street）has existed for decades.

简单句：一个主语Lao Jie（Old Street），一个谓语has existed。

◎Having the smell of countryside and nature, it was the only road there nearly half a century ago, which was a dirt lane and merged into its surrounding open fields.

复合句：一个主句it was the only road there nearly half a century ago；一个从句which was a dirt lane and merged into its surrounding open fields；同时这个从句中还有两个由and连接的并列分句was a dirt lane和merged into its surrounding open fields。

◎Having sped up since the 1980s, the change in China's urban landscape has been happening at an ever-increasing rate on an unprecedented scale.

简单句：一个主语the change，一个谓语has been happening。

◎In no time at all, the rural villages that once dotted the landscape had simply disappeared.

复合句：一个主句the rural villages had simply disappeared，一个从句that once dotted the landscape。

主从复合句点拨：无论是主句还是从句，叫作"句"就一定有谓语动词。从句

也是句子，判定是什么从句就看该从句在整个复合句中充当什么句子成分。如，定语从句就是该从句在整个复合句中作定语成分。定语从句，尤其是非限定性定语从句在英文表达中使用频率较高。

构词与常用搭配

exist（*v.*）存在：由词根sist（站，立足）加上前缀ex-=out（向外）构成；同根词还有：assist（协助），consist（并存）。

常用搭配：exist on，really exist

lane（*n.*）巷子：源自原始日耳曼语的lano（小巷，通道）。

常用搭配：country lanes，a muddy lane，a narrow lane，eastbound / westbound / southbound / northbound lanes

merge（*v.*）相融：源自一表示"浸没"的拉丁文。同根词还有：emerge（浮现），immerge（浸没），submerge（沉没）。

常用搭配：merge into，merge together，merge with，merge to

surrounding（*a.*）包围的；周围的：由词根und=water（und拼写受round的俗化影响）加上前缀sur-（超越），再加上形容词后缀-ing构成，原义："水溢出"，引申为"周围"。

常用搭配：surrounding area，surrounding land，surrounding fields，surrounding trees，surrounding buildings，surrounding scenery

urban（*a.*）城市的：由词根urb=city（城市）加上形容词后缀-an构成。同根词有：suburb（市郊）。

常用搭配：urban population，urban resident，urban and rural，urban life，urban areas

landscape（*n.*）风景：由词根scape=shape（专指"自然风景画"）加上名词land（陆地）构成复合名词。引申为"景色"。

常用搭配：desert landscape，landscape painting，garden landscape

unprecedented（*a.*）无先例的：由词根ced=go（前进；行走）加上前缀pre-（前，先）再加上否定前缀un-，和名词后缀-ent，形容词后缀-ed构成的。

常用搭配：unprecedented step，unprecedented level，unprecedented success，unprecedented rate，unprecedented challenges，unprecedented spectacle，unprecedented scale

scale（n.）规模：该词原义是"鳞"，后经过衍生引申为"状如鳞的事物"：刻度、比例、规模、程度、范围、梯子、水垢等等。

常用搭配：global scale，large scale，small scale，massive scale，grand scale，huge scale

rural（a.）农村的：由词根rus（开阔地）加上形容词后缀-al（……的）构成。

常用搭配：rural areas，rural economy，rural district，rural highway，rural population，rural region，rural resident，

Crossword Puzzle

Across

6. having never happened, been done or been known before

9. a narrow road in the country

10. the differences between two things gradually disappear so that it is impossible to separate them

Down

1. being covered in dots

2. relating to or concerned with a city or densely populated area

3. to be near or around something

4. everything you can see when you look across a large area of land

5. the size or extent of something, especially when compared with something else

7. to be real; to be present in a place or situation

8. connected with or like the countryside

Extraordinary Changes of E-commerce in China 中国电子商务的卓越变化

There are extraordinary changes of E-commerce in China. The electronic payment such as Alipay or WeChat is so popular that paper currency only be used occasionally. Wearing yellow jackets, the Meituan deliverers are frequently seen shuttling down streets, and thus makes online food ordering amazingly convenient and fast. In the same way, Taobao, an online shopping website makes online purchasing items widely accepted and beloved. With Didi, a taxi-hailing app, tailored taxi services have become hot. The pace of life is becoming quicker and quicker as E-commerce technology rapidly develops.

Reading Comprehension

Background Information

电子商务是我国这几年发展起来的标志产业。目前，我国的电子商务市场占有全世界40％以上的在线零售交易额。我国的电子商务在以每年27％的速度增长。政府出台的"互联网+政策"更是集"高速稳定增长"与"高效有效管理"两轮驱动于一体，从而进一步推升电子商务领域的稳健起飞。至今我国已打造出全球最先进的电子商务生态系统。中国经济转型发展和腾飞的轨迹是与中国电子商务的兴盛息息相关的。梳理电子商务发展的历史就可以看到中国经济高速发展的脉络。

Critical Thinking

Question One：What are the leading factors of rapid development of E-commerce in China?

Question Two：What else will the extraordinary changes of E-commerce bring China?

Question Three：What are the pros and cons of E-commerce? Will paper money be completely replaced by electronic money? Why or why not?

Language Focus

英语句子结构上具有后开放性特点，因此在使用英语表达时应该先将句子的主干提取出来，最后再添上句子的其他附加成分。

句子主干 指的是构成一个完整句子的框架，主要包括几个基本句子成分：主语、谓语、宾语、表语。

本语篇一共由6个句子构成，它们的句子主干分别是：

☆There are changes.

☆The payment is popular.

☆Deliverers are seen，and thus makes ordering convenient and fast.

☆Taobao makes purchasing accepted and beloved.

☆Services have become hot.

☆The pace is becoming quicker and quicker.

句子附加成分 指的是去除一个完整句子中的主干部分剩余的修饰、补充说明部分，主要包括几个基本句子成分：定语、状语、宾语补足语、主语补足语、同位语、插入语。

本语篇的句子附加成分如下：

★extraordinary（形容词作定语）

★of E-commerce（介词短语作后置定语）

★in China（介词短语作状语）

★electronic（形容词作定语）

★such as Alipay or WeChat（短语介词引出插入语）

★so（程度副词作状语）

★that paper currency only be used occasionally（结果状语从句）

★Wearing yellow jackets（现在分词短语作状语，表主动、表伴随、表进行）

★the Meituan（名词作定语）

★frequently（副词作状语）

★shuttling down streets（现在分词短语作主语补足语，表进行）

★online food（名词短语作定语）

★amazingly（副词作状语）

★In the same way（介词短语作状语）

★an online shopping website（名词短语作同位语）

★online（名词作定语）

★items（名词作宾语）

★ widely（副词作状语）

★ With Didi（介词短语作状语）

★ a taxi-hailing app（名词短语作同位语）

★ tailored taxi（名词短语作定语）

★ of life（介词短语作后置定语）

★ as E-commerce technology rapidly develops（伴随状语从句）

非谓语动词 是指动词在句子中不作谓语时的形式，因此它不受主语的限制。非谓语动词在英语句子中使用频繁且广泛。它可以在句子中充当除了谓语之外的其他成分，主语、宾语、表语、定语、状语、补语等。非谓语动词分为3大类：

◆ 动词不定式：to do / to be

◆ 动名词：doing / being

◆ 分词，一个是现在分词：doing / being；另一个是过去分词：done / been。

本语篇中非谓语动词的使用：

◇ **wearing** yellow jackets 现在分词短语作状语表进行、伴随

◇ frequently seen **shuttling down** streets 现在分词短语作主语补足语表正在进行

◇ makes online food **ordering** amazingly convenient and fast 动名词短语作宾语

◇ an online **shopping** website 动名词作定语，表示所修饰名词的功能、属性

◇ makes online **purchasing** items widely accepted and beloved 动名词短语作宾语

◇ With Didi，a **taxi-hailing** app 复合动名词作定语，表示所修饰名词的功能、属性

◇ **tailored** taxi services 过去分词作定语表被动、完成

句子类型 主要包括：简单句、复合句和并列句。在用英文表达时，尽量得体、恰当地交叉使用它们。简单句是指，一个主语或者两个、多个并列主语加上一个谓语或者两个、多个并列谓语构成的句子。复合句是指，一个主句加上一个或者多个从句构成的句子。并列句是指，由并列连词把两个或多个简单句连在一起构成的句子。

本语篇中句子类型的使用：

◎ There are extraordinary changes of E-commerce in China.

简单句：一个主语changes，一个谓语are。

◎The electronic payment such as Alipay or WeChat is so popular that paper currency only be used occasionally.

复合句：一个主句The electronic payment such as Alipay or WeChat is so popular，一个从句that paper currency only be used occasionally。

◎Wearing yellow jackets，the Meituan deliverers are frequently seen shuttling down streets，and thus makes online food ordering amazingly convenient and fast.

并列句：由and连接两个并列分句，分句一是Wearing yellow jackets，the Meituan deliverers are frequently seen shuttling down streets，分句二是thus makes online food ordering amazingly convenient and fast。

◎In the same way，Taobao，an online shopping website makes online purchasing items widely accepted and beloved.

简单句：一个主语Taobao，一个谓语makes。

◎With Didi，a taxi-hailing app，tailored taxi services have become hot.

简单句：一个主语services，一个谓语have become。

◎The pace of life is becoming quicker and quicker as E-commerce technology rapidly develops.

复合句：一个主句The pace of life is becoming quicker and quicker，一个从句as E-commerce technology rapidly develops。

主从复合句点拨：无论是主句还是从句，叫作"句"就一定有谓语动词。从句也是句子，判定是什么从句就看该从句在整个复合句中充当什么句子成分。如，定语从句就是该从句在整个复合句中作定语成分。定语从句，尤其是非限定性定语从句在英文表达中使用频率较高。

构词与常用搭配

extraordinary（*a.*）非凡的：由词根ordin=order（顺序，秩序）加上形容词后缀-ary再加上前缀extra-（额外的）构成。

常用搭配：extraordinary things，extraordinary patience and endurance，extraordinary skill，extraordinary personality，extraordinary work

e-commerce（*n.*）电子商务：由词根merc=trade（贸易；商）加上前缀com-=together

（共同），再加上electronic的简写e-，合成"电子商务"。

常用搭配：e-commerce revenue，e-commerce platform，e-commerce site，e-commerce product，e-commerce industry

electronic（*a.*）电子的：由词根electr（电）加上表示"微小的"名词后缀-on，再加上形容词后缀-ic构成。

常用搭配：an electronic calculator，electronic music，electronic equipment，electronic form，an electronic device，electronic paying，electronic mail=email

currency（*n.*）流通货币：由词根cur=run（跑；流；快速做）加上名词后缀-ency构成。

常用搭配：foreign currency，local currency，currency exchange，currency traders

shuttle（*v.*）穿梭：源自原始日耳曼语的"投掷"，同源词还有：shut，shot，shoot。

常用搭配：shuttle back and forth，shuttle bus，shuttle service，the space shuttle

convenient（*a.*）便利的：由词根ven=come（来）加上前缀con-=together（一起），再加上形容词后缀-ent构成。

常用搭配：convenient source，convenient time，convenient excuse，convenient way，convenient transportation

hail（*v.*）打招呼：与holy，health同一个词源，源自古英语中表示"健康"的一个词。后引申为"欢呼"，即为祝福健康，长命百岁而赞颂，相当于"万岁"。

常用搭配：hail a taxi，taxi-hailing

tailored（*a.*）量身定做的：由词根tail（切）加上名词后缀-or（人），再变成过去分词作形容词用。

常用搭配：well tailored，carefully tailored，beautifully tailored，tailored suit，tailored training

Crossword Puzzle

Across

3. the metal or paper medium of exchange that is presently used

6. beyond what is ordinary or usual; highly unusual or exceptional or remarkable

8. in an amazing manner; to everyone's surprise

9. call for; to signal to a taxi or a bus, in order to get the driver to stop

10. made for a particular person or purpose

Down

1. very popular with somebody

2. the activity of buying and selling goods on the Internet

4. of or relating to electronics; concerned with or using devices that operate on principles governing the behavior of electrons

5. suited to your comfort or purpose or needs

7. travel back and forth between two points

Dramatic Changes of Yellow River in China 中国黄河的沧桑巨变

Due to climate change and unreasonable practices of water conservation and management, Yellow River in China, also known as the "Mother River", had been dry over 20 times within 27 years before measures were taken to prevent. After going through some radical changes during the past several decades, the river is much more reliable and safer than ever today. It has become the first big river to overcome the threat of drying-up in the world. It serves as a cradle for Chinese civilization.

Reading Comprehension

Background Information

"黄河宁，天下平。"黄河治理从古至今都是兴国安邦的一件大事，保护黄河是事关我国永续发展的千秋大计。让黄河成为造福人民的幸福河，必须要坚持源头防治、综合施策，强化水体差异化保护修复治理。"黄河生态系统是一个有机整体"，我们应该在这一原则的基础上，认清黄河上中下游的环境差异，分门别类地做好山水林田湖草沙一体化保护修复工作，维护黄河流域整体生态系统的健康。

Critical Thinking

Question One: What do you know about Yellow River Civilization from ancient times to the present day in China?

Question Two: What should successful and sustainable governance of the Yellow River contain?

Question Three: What are the reasons for dramatic changes of the Yellow River in China?

Language Focus

英语句子结构上具有后开放性特点，因此在使用英语表达时应该先将句子的主干提取出来，最后再添上句子的其他附加成分。

句子主干 指的是构成一个完整句子的框架，主要包括几个基本句子成分：主语、谓语、宾语、表语。

本语篇一共由4个句子构成，它们的句子主干分别是：

☆ Yellow River had been dry.

☆ The river is more reliable and safer.

☆It has become the river.

☆It serves.

句子附加成分 指的是去除一个完整句子中的主干部分剩余的修饰、补充说明部分，主要包括几个基本句子成分：定语、状语、宾语补足语、主语补足语、同位语、插入语。

本语篇的句子附加成分如下：

★Due to climate change and unreasonable practices（介词短语作原因状语）

★of water conservation and management（介词短语作后置定语）

★in China（介词短语作后置定语）

★also known as the "Mother River"（过去分词短语作插入语）

★over 20 times（介词短语作状语）

★within 27 years（介词短语作状语）

★before measures were taken to prevent（时间状语从句）

★After going through some radical changes（介词短语作状语）

★during the past several decades（介词短语作状语）

★much（程度副词作状语）

★ than ever today（由连词than引导省略了主语和谓语的比较状语从句）

★the first（序数词前加定冠词the作定语）

★big（形容词作定语）

★to overcome the threat（动词不定式短语作后置定语）

★of drying-up（介词短语作后置定语）

★in the world（介词短语作状语）

★as a cradle（介词短语作宾语）

★for Chinese civilization（介词短语作后置定语）

非谓语动词 是指动词在句子中不作谓语时的形式，因此它不受主语的限制。非谓语动词在英语句子中使用频繁且广泛。它可以在句子中充当除了谓语之外的其他成分，主语、宾语、表语、定语、状语、补语等。非谓语动词分为3大类：

◆动词不定式：to do／to be

◆动名词：doing／being

◆分词，一个是现在分词：doing/being；另一个是过去分词：done/been。

本语篇中非谓语动词的使用：

◇also **known as** the "Mother River" 过去分词短语作插入语表被动，有补充解释的作用

　　◇After **going** through some radical changes 动名词短语作宾语

　　◇**to overcome** the threat 动词不定式短语作后置定语

　　◇the threat of **drying-up** in the world 动名词作介词of的宾语

句子类型 主要包括：简单句、复合句和并列句。在用英文表达时，尽量得体、恰当地交叉使用它们。简单句是指，一个主语或者两个、多个并列主语加上一个谓语或者两个、多个并列谓语构成的句子。复合句是指，一个主句加上一个或者多个从句构成的句子。并列句是指，由并列连词把两个或多个简单句连在一起构成的句子。

本语篇中句子类型的使用：

◎Due to climate change and unreasonable practices of water conservation and management, Yellow River in China, also known as the "Mother River", had been dry over 20 times within 27 years before measures were taken to prevent.

复合句：一个主句Due to climate change and unreasonable practices of water conservation and management, Yellow River in China, also known as the "Mother River", had been dry over 20 times within 27 years, 一个从句before measures were taken to prevent。

◎After going through some radical changes during the past several decades, the river is much more reliable and safer than ever today.

简单句：一个主语the river，一个谓语，系表结构is more reliable and safer。

◎It has become the first big river to overcome the threat of drying-up in the world.

简单句：一个主语It，一个谓语has become。

◎It serves as a cradle for Chinese civilization.

简单句：一个主语It，一个谓语serves。

主从复合句点拨：无论是主句还是从句，叫作"句"就一定有谓语动词。从句也是句子，判定是什么从句就看该从句在整个复合句中充当什么句子成分。如，定

语从句就是该从句在整个复合句中作定语成分。定语从句，尤其是非限定性定语从句在英文表达中使用频率较高。

构词与常用搭配

dramatic（*a.*）戏剧性的；突然的；巨大的：由词根drama（戏剧）加上形容词性后缀-tic构成。

常用搭配：a dramatic increase / fall / change / improvement，dramatic results / developments / news，a dramatic effect，dramatic and exciting，a dramatic film

unreasonable（*a.*）不理智的：由词根reason加上形容词后缀-able（具有……能力的），再加上否定前缀un-构成。

常用搭配：unreasonable behavior，unreasonable increases，unreasonable rules，unreasonable demands，unreasonable action，unreasonable request，unreasonable regulations

conservation（*n.*）对自然环境的保护：由词根serv=serve=keep（保持），加上前缀con-=together（一起，全部），再加上名词后缀-ation构成。

常用搭配：energy conservation，conservation projects，water conservation，conservation and utilization，conservation of resources，wildlife conservation

radical（*a.*）根本的；彻底的：由词根radic=root（根）加上形容词后缀-al构成。

常用搭配：radical differences，radical ideas，radical changes，radical reform，radical transformation，radical policy，radical politician / students / writers（修饰人，指"激进的"），radical cure

reliable（*a.*）可靠的：由词根li=tie（捆绑）加上表示"重复"的前缀re-，再加上表示"具有……能力的"形容词后缀-able构成。

常用搭配：a reliable friend，a reliable source，reliable information，reliable system，reliable service，a reliable person，a reliable fellow，reliable evidence

overcome（*v.*）战胜：由词根come（来）加上前缀over-（在……上）构成。

常用搭配：overcome difficulties，overcome fear，overcome weakness，overcome defects

cradle（*n.*）摇篮：源于表示"编织；弯；转"的词汇，同源词还有：crib（婴儿床），ring（包围，环绕）。

常用搭配：the cradle of，from the cradle to the grave

Crossword Puzzle

Across

4. to succeed in dealing with or controlling a problem that has been preventing you from achieving something

6. the preservation and careful management of the environment and of natural resources

8. new, different and likely to have a great effect

9. exciting and impressive; thrilling in effect

Down

1. absurd and inappropriate

2. worthy of being depended on; can be trusted to do something well

3. the process of extracting moisture

5. a particular society at a particular time and place

7. the place where something originated or was nurtured in its early existence

A Huge Shopping Revolution 购物方式的巨大变化

A huge shopping revolution is taking place in China. Modern technology offers platforms for different shopping behaviors, which makes the e-commerce soar in China. China is a country of mobile commerce now owing to the technology platforms such as Alibaba, Tencent, Tik Tok and JD. Shopping is also embodied in different forms such as livestreamings and WeChat chatrooms. Almost everything is offered on the mobiles, from Luosifen to insurances products, as long as you can imagine. The ultraconvenience, speed and effectiveness of delivering promote online shopping behavior to be a habit. The delivery includes almost everything: ice-creams, vegetables and even Alaska king crabs. From China, we can get a glimpse into the future of shopping.

Reading Comprehension

Background Information

20世纪90年代以来，网络和信息技术有了突破性的进展。在网络普及的背景下，网络购物应运而生。1998年中国出现了第一笔网络购物。网购这一新兴的购物方式，具有强大的生命力，呈几何级增长。在此背景下，中国的企业经历了重要的发展阶段。一些传统企业，没有能够融入新的经营方式，被淘汰出局。一些企业结合网络平台，整合渠道，完善布局，给传统的企业带来了新的活力和发展方向。在中国，网络交易体系日渐完善，网络交易平台已经拥有了良好的商业运转模式。近年来，中国网民的数量不断地增加，网购的规模也在不断地上升。

Critical Thinking

Question One: There are many kinds of online products with uneven quality. As ordinary consumers, how can we ensure the quality of online products?

Question Two: What are the pros and cons of traditional shopping compared with online shopping?

Question Three: Bricks and mortar stores are hit hardly by online shopping. Is it necessary to adopt any methods to protect the bricks and mortar stores? How to do that?

Language Focus

英语句子结构上具有后开放性特点，因此在使用英语表达时应该先将句子的主干提取出来，最后再添上句子的其他附加成分。

句子主干 指的是构成一个完整句子的框架，主要包括几个基本句子成分：主语、谓语、宾语、表语。

本语篇一共由7个句子构成，它们的句子主干分别是：

☆A revolution is taking place.

☆Technology offers platforms.

☆China is a country.

☆Shopping is embodied.

☆Everything is offered.

☆The ultraconvenience，speed and effectiveness promote behavior to be a habit.

☆The delivery includes everything.

☆We can get a glimpse.

句子附加成分 指的是去除一个完整句子中的主干部分剩余的修饰、补充说明部分，主要包括几个基本句子成分：定语、状语、宾语补足语、主语补足语、同位语、插入语。

本语篇的句子附加成分如下：

★huge shopping（形容词和动名词作定语）

★in China（介词短语作地点状语）

★modern（形容词作定语）

★for different shopping behaviors（介词短语作地点补语）

★which makes the e-commerce soar in China.（非限定性定语从句）

★of mobile commerce（介词短语作后置定语）

★now（副词作状语）

★owing to the technology platforms such as Alibaba，Tencent，Tik Tok and JD（动名词短语作原因状语）

★also（副词作状语）

★in different forms（介词短语作状语）

★such as livestreamings and WeChat chatrooms（名词短语作补语）

★almost（副词作状语）

★on the mobiles（介词短语作状语）

★from Luosifen to insurances products（介词短语作补语）

★as long as you can imagine（条件状语从句）

★online shopping（名词短语作定语）

★ice-creams，vegetables and even Alaska king crabs（名词短语作补语）

★From China（介词短语作状语）

★into the future of shopping（介词短语作补语）

非谓语动词 是指动词在句子中不作谓语时的形式，因此它不受主语的限制。非谓语动词在英语句子中使用频繁且广泛。它可以在句子中充当除了谓语之外的其他成分，主语、宾语、表语、定语、状语、补语等。非谓语动词分为3大类：

◆动词不定式：to do / to be

◆动名词：doing / being

◆分词，一个是现在分词：doing / being；另一个是过去分词：done / been。

本语篇中非谓语动词的使用：

◇A huge **shopping** revolution 动名词作定语修饰名词，表示其性质。

◇makes the e-commerce **soar** in China 动词不定式（省略to）作宾语补足语。

◇**owing** to 现在分词加介词作状语表示原因、伴随、进行。

句子类型 主要包括：简单句、复合句和并列句。在用英文表达时，尽量得体、恰当地交叉使用它们。简单句是指，一个主语或者两个、多个并列主语加上一个谓语或者两个、多个并列谓语构成的句子。复合句是指，一个主句加上一个或者多个从句构成的句子。并列句是指，由并列连词把两个或多个简单句连在一起构成的句子。

本语篇中句子类型的使用：

◎A huge shopping revolution is taking place in China.

简单句：一个主语A revolution 一个谓语is taking place。

◎Modern technology offers platforms for different shopping behaviors，which makes the e-commerce soar in China.

复合句：一个主句Modern technology offers platforms for different shopping behaviors；一个从句which makes the e-commerce soar in China。

◎China is a country of mobile commerce now owing to the technology platforms such as Alibaba，Tencent，Tik Tok and JD.

简单句：主系表结构，一个主语 China，一个系动词is，一个表语 a country。

◎Shopping is also embodied in different forms such as livestreamings and WeChat chatrooms.

简单句：一个主语Shopping，一个谓语is embodied。

◎Almost everything is offered on the mobiles, from Luosifen to insurances products, as long as you can imagine.

复合句：一个主句Almost everything is offered on the mobiles, from Luosifen to insurances products，一个条件从句as long as you can imagine。

◎The ultraconvenience, speed and effectiveness of delivering promote online shopping behavior to be a habit.

简单句：三个并列主语The ultraconvenience, speed和effectiveness，一个谓语promote。

◎The delivery includes almost everything: ice-creams, vegetables and even Alaska king crabs.

简单句：一个主语The delivery，一个谓语includes。

◎From China, we can get a glimpse into the future of shopping.

简单句：一个主语we，一个谓语can get。

主从复合句点拨：无论是主句还是从句，叫作"句"就一定有谓语动词。从句也是句子，判定是什么从句就看该从句在整个复合句中充当什么句子成分。如，条件从句就是该从句在整个复合句中作状语成分。条件从句表示假如有从句的动作发生就（不）会有主句的动作发生。

构词与常用搭配

revolution（n.）革命：该词由前缀re-（再，重复）加上词根-volut-（卷动）和名词后缀 -ion 构成，翻天覆地的大变化引申为革命。

常用搭配：cultural revolution，industrial revolution，technological revolution

platform（n.）平台：该词源于来自古法语plat（平的）加上form（形成），引申为平台。

常用搭配：service platform，open platform，operating platform

commerce（n.）贸易，商业：由前缀 com-=tother（共同）加上词根 merc（商）构成。

常用搭配：electronic commerce，mobile commerce，Ministry of Commerce

embody（v.）具体体现：该词由前缀em-（进入，使）加上词根body（身体，具象）构成，引申为具体体现。

常用搭配：embody in，embody a high five，to embody

insurance（n.）保险：该词由前缀in-（向内）加上词根-sur-（确信）和名词后缀 -ance构成。

常用搭配：medical insurance，health insurance，social insurance

effectiveness（n.）有效：该词由前缀 ef-（=ex-出）加上词根 -fect-（做，作）和形容词词缀 -ive加上名词后缀ness构成。

常用搭配：cost effectiveness，advertising effectiveness，effectiveness theory

delivery（n.）递交：该词前缀de-（加强）加上词根-liver（=-liber-自由，释放）和后缀 -y构成。引申为投递，传送，递交之义。

常用搭配：delivery time，delivery system，express delivery，delivery service

Crossword Puzzle

Across

1. a drastic and far-reaching change in ways of thinking and behaving

3. a raised horizontal surface

5. represent in bodily form

6. the act of delivering or distributing something as goods or mail

7. promise of reimbursement in the case of loss

Down

2. power to be effective; the quality of being able to bring about an effect

4. transactions（sales and purchases）having the objective of supplying commodities

China's High-Speed Rail 中国高铁

China's high-speed rail, which started from the Beijing–Tianjin Intercity railway in 2008, continuously upgrades and sets new world records. China's high-speed railway network, called "four vertical and horizontal" with 40 thousand kilometers operating mileage at the end of 2021, ranks first in the world. Currently, there are four lines operating at 350 km/h in China: Beijing-Shanghai, Beijing–Tianjin intercity, Chengdu–Chongqing, and Beijing–Zhangjiakou (some sections). It used to take more than 13 hours to travel from Beijing to Wuhan by train 20 years ago. Now it is reduced to 4 hours and 17 minutes. Meanwhile China's high-speed trains are accessible for all income groups with favorable fares. China seems to be on track to a high-speed rail revolution.

Reading Comprehension

Background Information

中国内陆面积较大，人口众多，需要强大的运输体系连接整个国家和国民经济。铁路作为重要的交通方式，有非常多显著的优点：运载量大、成本低和耗能少。20世纪80年代兴建高铁的建议被提出。历经十几年的考察、分析和调研，1998年建设高速铁路成为全国人民代表大会"十五"计划纲要草案中最重要的提议之一。草案提出当年中国高铁发展进入预备阶段，直到2008年京津城际高速铁路开通标志着中国第一条高速铁路正式运营。它连接北京和天津两大城市，是我国第一条设计时速大于300km/h的高速铁路。至此，中国进入高铁时代。

Critical Thinking

Question One: What benefits does high-speed rail bring to our lives?

Question Two: What are the advantages of high-speed rail over airplanes?

Question Three: Under what circumstances would you choose a high-speed train over a plane?

Language Focus

英语句子结构上具有后开放性特点，因此在使用英语表达时应该先将句子的主干提取出来，最后再添上句子的其他附加成分。

句子主干 指的是构成一个完整句子的框架，主要包括几个基本句子成分：主语、谓语、宾语、表语。

本语篇一共由7个句子构成，它们的句子主干分别是：

☆ High-speed rail upgrades and sets records.

☆ Network ranks first.

☆ There are lines

☆ It used to take hours.

☆ It is reduced.

☆ Trains are accessible.

☆ China seems to be on track.

句子附加成分 指的是去除一个完整句子中的主干部分剩余的修饰、补充说明部分，主要包括几个基本句子成分：定语、状语、宾语补足语、主语补足语、同位语、插入语。

本语篇的句子附加成分如下：

★ China's（名词所有格作定语）

★ which started from the Beijing–Tianjin Intercity railway in 2008（非限定性定语从句）

★ continuously（副词作状语）

★ new world（名词短语作定语）

★ China's high-speed railway（名词短语作定语）

★ called "four vertical and horizontal" with 40 thousand kilometers operating mileage at the end of 2021（动词过去分词短语作插入语）

★ in the world（介词短语作状语）

★ Currently（副词作状语）

★ four（数词作定语）

★ operating at 350 km/h in China（动名词短语作后置定语）

★ Beijing–Shanghai，Beijing-Tianjin intercity，Chengdu–Chongqing，and Beijing–Zhangjiakou（some sections）（名词短语作补语）

★ more than 13（名词短语作定语）

★ to travel（动词不定式短语作定语）

★ from Beijing to Wuhan（介词短语作地点状语）

★ by train（介词短语作方式状语）

★20 years ago（名词短语作时间状语）

★Now（副词作状语）

★to 4 hours and 17 minutes（介词短语作主语补语）

★Meanwhile（副词作状语）

★China's high-speed（名词短语作定语）

★for all income groups with favorable fares（介词短语作方式状语）

★on track（介词短语作be动词的表语）

★to a high-speed rail revolution（动词不定式作后置定语）

非谓语动词 是指动词在句子中不作谓语时的形式，因此它不受主语的限制。非谓语动词在英语句子中使用频繁且广泛。它可以在句子中充当除了谓语之外的其他成分，主语、宾语、表语、定语、状语、补语等。非谓语动词分为3大类：

◆动词不定式：to do / to be

◆动名词：doing / being

◆分词，一个是现在分词：doing / being；另一个是过去分词：done / been。

本语篇中非谓语动词的使用：

◇**to take** more than 13 hours 动词不定式作主语补足语

◇**to travel** from Beijing to Wuhan 动词不定式作宾语补足语

◇**to be** on track 动词不定式作状语，表示结果

句子类型 主要包括：简单句、复合句和并列句。在用英文表达时，尽量得体、恰当地交叉使用它们。简单句是指，一个主语或者两个、多个并列主语加上一个谓语或者两个、多个并列谓语构成的句子。复合句是指，一个主句加上一个或者多个从句构成的句子。并列句是指，由并列连词把两个或多个简单句连在一起构成的句子。

本语篇中句子类型的使用：

◎China's high-speed rail, which started from the Beijing–Tianjin Intercity railway in 2008, continuously upgrades and sets new world records.

复合句：一个主句China's high-speed rail continuously upgrades and sets new world records；一个从句which started from the Beijing–Tianjin Intercity railway in 2008。

◎China's high-speed railway network, called "four vertical and horizontal" with 40 thousand kilometers operating mileage at the end of 2021, ranks first in the world.

简单句：一个主语network，一个谓语ranks。

◎Currently，there are four lines operating at 350 km/h in China：Beijing-Shanghai，Beijing–Tianjin intercity，Chengdu–Chongqing，and Beijing–Zhangjiakou（some sections）．

简单句：There be句型中，一个主语lines，一个谓语are。

◎It used to take more than 13 hours to travel from Beijing to Wuhan by train 20 years ago.

简单句：一个主语It，一个谓语used to take，一个宾语hours。

◎Now it is reduced to 4 hours and 17 minutes.

简单句：一个主语it，一个谓语is reduced。

◎Meanwhile China's high-speed trains are accessible for all income groups with favorable fares.

简单句：一个主语China's high-speed trains，一个谓语 are。

◎China seems to be on track to a high-speed rail revolution.

简单句：一个主语China，一个谓语seems。

主从复合句点拨：无论是主句还是从句，叫作"句"就一定有谓语动词。从句也是句子，判定是什么从句就看该从句在整个复合句中充当什么句子成分。如，定语从句就是该从句在整个复合句中作定语成分。定语从句，尤其是非限定性定语从句在英文表达中使用频率较高，它对主句中某一个词或者整个主句起到补充说明作用。

构词与常用搭配

upgrade（v.）提升：由前缀up（向上）加上词根grad（步，级）构成。

常用搭配：upgrade kit，upgrade oneself，on the upgrade

vertical（a.）垂直的：vertex，顶点，加上形容词后缀-cal引申为垂直的。

常用搭配：vertical limit，vertical direction，vertical distribution

horizontal（a.）水平的：该词源自希腊语horizon（地平线），加上形容词后缀-al构成。

常用搭配：horizontal direction，horizontal line，horizontal bar

mileage（n.）英里数：该词由词根mile-（英里）加上名词后缀-age构成。

常用搭配：gas mileage，mileage recorder，mileage charges

reduce（v.）减少，还原：该词由前缀re-（回）加上词根duc（引导）构成。含义为向后引导，引申为缩退，还原，减少。

常用搭配：reduce pollution，reduce weight，reduce waste

accessible（*a.*）易接近的，可到达的：该词由前缀 ac-（来，临近）加上词根 cess（行走）和形容词后缀 -ible 构成，含有被动意义。

常用搭配：readily accessible，accessible point，accessible surface

income（*n.*）收入：该词由前缀 in-（内）加上词根 come（来）构成。

常用搭配：income tax，income gap，income distribution

track（*n.*）轨道：该词源于古法语 trac（轨迹，车道）。

常用搭配：on track，keep track，track and field

Crossword Puzzle

Across

5. lower in grade or rank or force somebody into an undignified situation

6. easily obtained

7. a pair of parallel rails providing a runway for wheels

Down

1. parallel to or in the plane of the horizon or a base line

2. the financial gain (earned or unearned) accruing over a given period of time

3. distance measured in miles

4. at a right angle to another line or plane, or to the earth's surface

Rural Revitalization in China 中国乡村振兴

In the late 1970s, China began the rural reform. China has been advancing a new round of rural reform to ensure rural development and farmers' well-being. Many effective measures have been adopted, such as promoting transfer of farmland management rights, facilitating rural financial support and improving training for new-generation farmers. In 2020, China has eradicated absolute poverty and now is focusing on the comprehensive promotion of rural revitalization. Villages across the country are exploring their unique characteristics and best way to achieve prosperity, such as rural tourism, shared farm, industry and E-commerce.

Reading Comprehension

Background Information

民以食为天，粮食是最基本的生活资料，农业是人类食物之源，生存的根本。中国14亿人口的粮食、蔬菜、水果和肉类等食物，大多来自本国农业，农村是民生的重要基地。在我国，农业对经济的发展和国家的稳定起着重要的作用，新农村建设得到了全国人民的关注。近年来在党和国家的领导下，农业综合生产能力飞速提升，农民收入不断增长，农村民生显著改善，农村面貌焕然一新。

Critical Thinking

Question One: What are the problems the new generation rural residents confront with? What preferential policies would famers like governments to provide with?

Question Two: How will you explain the phenomenon "Low prices for grain hurt the peasants"? What measures should be taken?

Question Three: If you are in charge of villages' development, what will you prioritize to do? Why?

Language Focus

英语句子结构上具有后开放性特点，因此在使用英语表达时应该先将句子的主干提取出来，最后再添上句子的其他附加成分。

句子主干 指的是构成一个完整句子的框架，主要包括几个基本句子成分：主语、谓语、宾语、表语。

本语篇一共由5个句子构成，它们的句子主干分别是：

☆China began the reform.

☆China has been advancing a reform.

☆Measures have been adopted.

☆China has eradicated poverty and is focusing on the promotion.

☆Villages are exploring characteristics and way.

句子附加成分 指的是去除一个完整句子中的主干部分剩余的修饰、补充说明部分，主要包括几个基本句子成分：定语、状语、宾语补足语、主语补足语、同位语、插入语。

本语篇的句子附加成分如下：

★in the late 1970s（介词短语作时间状语）

★rural（形容词作定语）

★new round of（名词短语作定语）

★to ensure rural development and farmers' well-being（动词不定式短语作状语）

★many effective（形容词短语作定语）

★such as promoting transfer of farmland management rights，facilitating rural financial support and improving training for new-generation farmers（名词短语作补语）

★in 2020（介词短语作时间状语）

★absolute（形容词作定语）

★now（副词作状语）

★comprehensive（形容词作定语）

★of rural revitalization（介词短语作定语）

★across the country（介词短语作定语）

★their unique（形容词短语作定语）

★best（形容词作定语）

★to achieve prosperity（动词不定式短语作状语）

★such as rural tourism，shared farm，industry and E-commerce（名词短语作补语）

★small-scale（名词作定语）

★modern agricultural production（名词短语作定语）

非谓语动词 是指动词在句子中不作谓语时的形式，因此它不受主语的限制。非谓语动词在英语句子中使用频繁且广泛。它可以在句子中充当除了谓语之外的其他

成分，主语、宾语、表语、定语、状语、补语等。非谓语动词分为3大类：

◆动词不定式：to do/to be

◆动名词：doing/being

◆分词，一个是现在分词：doing/being；另一个是过去分词：done/been。

本语篇中非谓语动词的使用：

◇**to ensure** rural development and farmers' well-being 动词不定式短语作状语表目的

◇**promoting** transfer of farmland management rights，**facilitating** rural financial support and **improving** training for new-generation farmers 动名词作介词宾语

◇best way **to achieve** prosperity 动词不定式短语作定语表未来要发生

句子类型 主要包括：简单句、复合句和并列句。在用英文表达时，尽量得体、恰当地交叉使用它们。简单句是指，一个主语或者两个、多个并列主语加上一个谓语或者两个、多个并列谓语构成的句子。复合句是指，一个主句加上一个或者多个从句构成的句子。并列句是指，由并列连词把两个或多个简单句连在一起构成的句子。

本语篇中句子类型的使用：

◎In the late 1970s，China began the rural reform.

简单句：一个主语China，一个谓语began，一个宾语reform。

◎China has been advancing a new round of rural reform to ensure rural development and farmers' well-being.

简单句：一个主语China，一个谓语has been advancing，一个宾语reform。

◎Many effective measures have been adopted，such as promoting transfer of farmland management rights，facilitating rural financial support and improving training for new-generation farmers.

简单句：一个主语measures，一个谓语has been adopted。

◎In 2020，China has eradicated absolute poverty and now is focusing on the comprehensive promotion of rural revitalization.

简单句：一个主语China，两个谓语has eradicated和is focusing。

◎Villages across the country are exploring their unique characteristics and best way to achieve prosperity，such as rural tourism，shared farm，industry and E-commerce.

简单句：一个主语Villages，一个谓语 are exploring，两个宾语characteristics and way。

简单句点拨：简单句的理解和运用主要需要抓住主语的关键词和谓语的核心词，厘清主谓之间的逻辑关系才能明确其含义。简单句在英文表达中也经常被使用。

构词与常用搭配

rural（*a.*）农村的：该词源自拉丁语 ruralis（乡村的），同源词是 room，rustic。

常用搭配：rural area，rural population，rural economics

reform（*n.*）改革：由前缀re-（再）加上词根form（形）构成，引申为改革之义。

常用搭配：curriculum reform，educational reform，deepen the reform

advance（*v / n.*）前进：该词源自拉丁语 abante，前缀 ab（从，从……离开）加上词根 ante（前面的）构成，即前进。

常用搭配：in advance，advance in，advance with times

measure（*n.*）测量、方法：该词源自古法语 mesurer（测量、检测），同源词有 meter，commensurate。

常用搭配：effective measure，technical measure，beyond measure

adopt（*v.*）采纳，收养：该词由前缀 ad-（去，往）加上词根 opt（选择）构成。引申含义、采纳、采取、收养。

常用搭配：adopt various methods，adopt an idea，adopt a new approach

promote（*v.*）促进、提升：该词由前缀pro-（前）加上词根mot（移动）和词末字母 -e 构成，引申为促进，提升，发扬。

常用搭配：promote sales，promote reform，promote cooperation

improve（*v.*）改进，改善：该词源自诺曼法语 emprouwer（使变成利润，增加收入），由前缀em-（进入，使）加上词根 prou（利润，收益）和词末字母-wer构成。引申为改进，改善。

常用搭配：improve efficiency，improve in，improve health

eradicate（*v.*）根除：由前缀e-（出，向外）加上词根 radic（根）和动词后缀-ate 构成。

常用搭配：eradicate illness，eradicate weeds，eradicate odor

comprehensive（*a.*）理解的、广泛的：由前缀com-全部+词根prehens 抓住+-ive形容词词尾构成。

常用搭配：comprehensive treatment，comprehensive income，comprehensive quality

Crossword Puzzle

Across

3. a change for the better as a result of correcting abuses

4. get better

5. take up and practice as one's own

6. move forward, also in the metaphorical sense

7. the act or process of assigning numbers to phenomena according to a rule

Down

1. destroy completely, as if down to the roots

2. contribute to the progress or growth of

8. living in or characteristic of farming or country life

Mobile Payment in China 中国移动支付

With a single mobile phone and a code or face scan, a contactless transaction can be done in an unprecedented way of payment—mobile payment. Now mobile payment has already become a new trend in the way Chinese people pay. Today, in most areas of China, people can use mobile payment for travel, service and daily expenses, which is convenient, quick, environmental and sanitary. People can pay without cash for a whole year, but it is difficult to pay without mobiles for a single day. According to the report released by China UnionPay on January 26, 2022, mobile payment accounts for more than 80% of consumption.

Reading Comprehension

Background Information

随着科技的进步，传统的现金和刷卡的支付方式逐渐被人舍弃，移动支付以其特有的优势慢慢地渗透到支付市场。人民对方便性和快捷性的追求越来越高，而现金和刷卡都稍显麻烦。现在人们对手机的依赖性非常高，手机可以解决非常多的问题。随着手机使用的普及，移动支付也在不断扩大。在当今中国，移动支付已经成为主要的支付方式。只要有手机、有网络，几乎随时随地点击下手机或者刷一下脸，就可以完成支付。

Critical Thinking

Question One: Mobile payment has brought a lot of convenience to people's life, but there are also many problems, such as payment security and account security. What can we ordinary people do to prevent them?

Question Two: From the perspective of government, what measures can be taken to prevent network fraud?

Question Three: What are the potential problems and impacts of mobile payment?

Language Focus

英语句子结构上具有后开放性特点，因此在使用英语表达时应该先将句子的主干提取出来，最后再添上句子的其他附加成分。

句子主干 指的是构成一个完整句子的框架，主要包括几个基本句子成分：主语、谓语、宾语、表语。

本语篇一共由5个句子构成，它们的句子主干分别是：

☆A transaction can be done.

☆Mobile payment has become a trend.

☆People can use mobile payment.

☆People can pay but it is difficult to pay.

☆Mobile payment accounts for consumption.

句子附加成分 指的是去除一个完整句子中的主干部分剩余的修饰、补充说明部分，主要包括几个基本句子成分：定语、状语、宾语补足语、主语补足语、同位语、插入语。

本语篇的句子附加成分如下：

★With a single mobile phone and a code or face scan（介词短语作状语）

★contactless（形容词作定语）

★in an unprecedented way of payment—mobile payment（介词短语作状语）

★now（副词作时间状语）

★already（副词作状语）

★new（形容词作定语）

★in the way Chinese people pay（介词短语作状语）

★Today（副词作时间状语）

★in most areas of China（介词短语作地点状语）

★for travel, service and daily expenses（介词短语作补语）

★which is convenient, quick, environmental and sanitary（非限定性定语从句）

★without cash for a whole year（介词短语作状语）

★without mobiles for a single day（介词短语作状语）

★According to the report released by China UnionPay（介词短语作状语）

★on January 26, 2022（介词短语作时间状语）

★for more than 80% of consumption（介词短语作补语）

非谓语动词 是指动词在句子中不作谓语时的形式，因此它不受主语的限制。非谓语动词在英语句子中使用频繁且广泛。它可以在句子中充当除了谓语之外的其他成分，主语、宾语、表语、定语、状语、补语等。非谓语动词分为3大类：

◆动词不定式：to do / to be

◆动名词：doing / being

◆分词，一个是现在分词：doing / being；另一个是过去分词：done / been。

本语篇中非谓语动词的使用：

◇an **unprecedented** way 过去分词作定语表示的含义有被动、完成。

◇**to pay** without mobiles 动词不定式短语作句子真正的主语。

◇the report **released** by China UnionPay 过去分词作定语表示的含义有被动、完成。

句子类型 主要包括：简单句、复合句和并列句。在用英文表达时，尽量得体、恰当地交叉使用它们。简单句是指，一个主语或者两个、多个并列主语加上一个谓语或者两个、多个并列谓语构成的句子。复合句是指，一个主句加上一个或者多个从句构成的句子。并列句是指，由并列连词把两个或多个简单句连在一起构成的句子。

本语篇中句子类型的使用：

◎With a single mobile phone and a code or face scan, a contactless transaction can be done in an unprecedented way of payment—mobile payment.

简单句：一个主语a transaction，一个谓语can be done。

◎Now mobile payment has already become a new trend in the way Chinese people pay.

简单句：一个主语mobile payment，一个谓语 has become。

◎Today, in most areas of China, people can use mobile payment for travel, service and daily expenses, which is convenient, quick, environmental and sanitary.

复合句：一个主句Today, in most areas of China, people can use mobile payment for travel, service and daily expenses；一个从句 which is convenient, quick, environmental and sanitary。

◎People can pay without cash for a whole year, but it is difficult to pay without mobiles for a single day.

并列句：由并列连词but把两个简单句 People can pay without cash for a whole year 和it is difficult to pay without mobiles for a single day连在一起。

◎According to the report released by China UnionPay on January 26, 2022, mobile payment accounts for more than 80% of consumption.

简单句：一个主语mobile payment，一个谓语accounts for。

并列句点拨：以连词and，not only...but also，but，however，while，yet，so等连接两个或者多个简单句构成的句子，叫作并列句。并列句分为联合并列句、转折并列句、选择并列句、因果并列句。例如，由转折连词but，while，yet，however等转折连词连接的两个简单句，表示两个句子之间有转折的含义。

构词与常用搭配

code（*n.*）密码：该词源于拉丁词 codex，树干，医典，账本。可能因古代树干上的文字比较难懂，引申词义密码。

常用搭配：zip code，postal code，source code

scan（*n.*）浏览、扫描：该词源于拉丁语 scandere（攀爬，攀登），引申词义仔细看，检查，浏览，后用于指扫描。同源词是ascend，descend。

常用搭配：skim and scan，body scan，CT scan

transaction（*n.*）交易、处理：由前缀trans-（转变）加上词根act（行动）和名词后缀 -ion 构成。

常用搭配：business transaction，transaction volume，transaction tax

unprecedented（*a.*）史无前例的：该词由否定前缀un（不）加上前缀pre-（前，先）和词根ced（行走）和后缀-ent 和形容词后缀-ed构成。

常用搭配：at an unprecedented rate，reach an unprecedented height

trend（*n.*）潮流、趋势：该词源于古英语trendan（滚动，转动），引申词义潮流，趋势。

常用搭配：market trend，development trend，linear trend

convenient（*a.*）方便的：该词由前缀con-（共同）加词根ven（来）和形容词后缀-ient 构成。

常用搭配：convenient and efficient，be convenient for，be convenient to do，convenient store

sanitary（*a.*）清洁的、卫生的：该词源自拉丁语sanus，健康的，与sane同源。引申词义清洁的，卫生的。

常用搭配：sanitary conditions，sanitary facilities，sanitary cup

release（*v.*）释放、发布：该词源自拉丁语，由前缀re-（回）和词根 laxare（放松，松弛）构成relaxare（放松，松弛），之后在古法语中将relaisser派生为 release。

常用搭配：release from，news release，heat release，stress release

consumption（*n.*）消费：该词由前缀con-（共同）加上词根sumpt（拿，买）和名词后缀-ion构成。

常用搭配：current consumption，power consumption，energy consumption，consumption tax

Crossword Puzzle

Across

5. having no precedent; never having happened, been done or been known before

7. allow to go; set free or liberate somebody/something

8. free from dirt or substances that may cause disease; hygienic

9. the act of transacting within or between groups（as carrying on commercial activities）

Down

1. suited to your comfort or purpose or needs

2. a general direction in which something tends to move

3. examine minutely or intensely

4. concerned with the ecological effects of altering the environment

6.（system of）words，letter，symbols etc. that represent others，used for secret messages or for presenting or recording information

Positive Changes in China's Fitness Industry 中国健身行业的积极变化

With the development of Internet technology, China's fitness industry has witnessed tremendous changes. Great efforts have been made to advance its national fitness program, energize new business models and allow people to socialize through exercise. In the past year, it is estimated that over 23 million users uploaded short clips related to exercise on Kuaishou, a leading short-video platform in China, and a daily average of more than 20 million users take live-streaming fitness courses on the platform.

Reading Comprehension

Background Information

受益于健康意识和收入水平的提高,全球健身市场规模保持稳健成长。信息技术促使健身产业进入互联网时代,为人们提供了个性化服务和社交功能。一些健身企业正在引领健身行业进行新业态变革。互联网通过更多的方式融入健身领域,越来越多的百姓积极参与到健康活动中来。同时,人与人、点对点的互动健身模式也打破了大众传统的健康理念、运动健身模式规则。

Critical Thinking

Question One: What do you think of online fitness industry? Are you crazy about keeping fit? Have you ever tried losing weight? Why are people keen on body shaping?

Question Two: What do you think of socializing through exercise online? Would you like to become a cyberstar coach of body shaping?

Question Three: What may be the main reasons why Chinese people are fond of keeping fit apps and body shaping?

Language Focus

英语句子结构上具有后开放性特点,因此在使用英语表达时应该先将句子的主干提取出来,最后再添上句子的其他附加成分。

句子主干 指的是构成一个完整句子的框架,主要包括主语、谓语、宾语、表语等基本句子成分。

本语篇一共由3个句子构成,它们的句子主干分别是:

☆Industry has witnessed changes.

☆Efforts have been made.

☆It is estimated.

句子附加成分 指的是去除一个完整句子中的主干部分剩余的修饰、补充说明部分，主要包括定语、状语、宾语补足语、主语补足语、同位语、插入语这几个基本句子成分。

本语篇的句子附加成分如下：

★ with the development（介词短语作原因状语）

★ of internet technology（介词短语作定语）

★ China's（名词所有格作定语）

★ fitness（名词作定语）

★ tremendous（形容词作定语）

★ great（形容词作定语）

★ national（形容词作定语）

★ new（形容词作定语）

★ business（名词作定语）

★ through exercise（介词短语作状语）

★ in the past year（介词短语作时间状语）

★ over（副词作状语）

★ 23 million（数量词作定语）

★ short（形容词作定语）

★ related to exercise（介词短语作定语）

★ on Kuaishou（介词短语作状语）

★ a short-video platform（名词短语作插入语）

★ In China（介词短语作定语）

★ leading（形容词作定语）

★ an average of（名词词组作定语）

★ more than（形容词作定语）

★ 20 million（数量词作定语）

★ on the platform（介词短语作状语）

非谓语动词 是指动词形式有一定的变换，在句子中不作谓语，因此它不受主语的限制。非谓语动词在英语中很常见。它可以在句子中充当主语、宾语、表语、定语、状语、补语等句子成分。非谓语动词有以下三种形式：

◆动词不定式：to do/to be

◆动名词：doing/being

◆分词，一个是现在分词：doing/being；另一个是过去分词：done/been。

本语篇中非谓语动词的使用：

◇to **advance** program，**energize** models and **allow** people to socialize 不定式短语作状语，表示目的

句子类型 主要包括简单句、复合句和并列句。在用英文表达时，尽量得体、恰当地交叉使用它们。简单句是指，一个主语或者两个以上主语加上一个谓语或者两个以上谓语构成的句子。复合句是指，一个主句加上一个或者多个从句构成的句子。并列句是指，两个以上简单句由并列连词连在一起构成的句子。

本语篇中句子类型的使用：

◎With the development of Internet technology，China's fitness industry has witnessed tremendous changes.

简单句：一个主语 fitness industry，一个谓语has witnessed。

◎Great efforts have been made to advance its national fitness program，energize new business models and allow people to socialize through exercise.

简单句：一个主语great efforts，一个谓语have been made。

◎In the past year，it is estimated that over 23 million users uploaded short clips related to exercise on Kuaishou，a leading short-video platform in China，and a daily average of more than 20 million users take live-streaming fitness courses on the platform.

复合句：一个主句it is estimated，一个从句：由that引导的主语从句over 23 million users uploaded short clips related to exercise on Kuaishou，a leading short-video platform in China，and a daily average of more than 20 million users take live-streaming fitness courses on the platform。

主从复合句点拨：无论是主句还是从句，叫作"句"就一定有谓语动词。从句也是句子，判定是什么从句就看该从句在整个复合句中充当什么句子成分。例如，主语从句就是该从句在整个复合句中作主语成分。主语从句通常被it代替作形

式主语，长长的主语从句移到句子后面，目的是保持句子结构的平衡——避免头重脚轻。

构词与常用搭配

fitness（*n.*）健康：由fit 适合的+名词词尾-ness构成

常用搭配：fitness club，health and fitness，fitness craze

positive（*a.*）积极的：由posit 放置+-ive 形容词词尾构成。

常用搭配：positive effect，positive thoughts，positive results

witness（*v.*）目击：由wit（vid）看见+-ness 名词词尾构成。

常用搭配：witness testimony，witness a signature

tremendous（*a.*）巨大的：由trem 发抖+-end 名词词尾+-ous 形容词词尾构成。

常用搭配：a tremendous amount of，tremendous pressure

energize（*v.*）激发：由en-加强意义+erg 工作，行动+-ize 动词词尾构成。

常用搭配：energize yourself，energize the city

socialize（*v.*）交际：由soci-联合+-al 形容词词尾+-ize 动词词尾构成。

常用搭配：socialized economy，socialize with

upload（*v.*）上传：由up与load构成的合成词。

常用搭配：upload a picture，upload function

estimate（*v.*）估计：该词来自拉丁语aestimare。

常用搭配：It's estimated that...

platform（*n.*）平台，来自古法语 plat，平的，form，形成。

常用搭配：multimedia platform，oil platform

live stream（*v.*）线上直播：由live（现场的）和stream（在线收看）构成的合成词。

常用搭配：live streaming radio

Crossword Puzzle

Across

3. full of hope and confidence, or giving cause for hope and confidence

6. very great in amount or level, or extremely good

9. to spend time when you are not working with friends or with other people in order to enjoy yourself

10. to see something happen, especially an accident or crime

Down

1. the condition of being physically strong and healthy

2. to broadcast video and sound of an event over the internet as it happens, or to be broadcast in this way

4. to make someone feel energetic or eager

5. to guess or calculate the cost, size, value, etc. of something

7. to copy or move programs or information to a larger computer system or to the internet

8. an opportunity to make your ideas or beliefs known publicly

Remarkable Changes of Space Exploration in China 中国空间探索的非凡之变

The space industry is a critical part of the country's overall strategy. China's space industry has produced a remarkable scorecard this year which is characterized by the nation's first independent Mars mission, the completion of a global navigation satellite network and a landmark adventure that retrieved rocks and soil from the moon. In the next five years, China will integrate space science, technology and application while adhering to the new development concept, building a new development model and meeting the requirements of high-quality development. China's space industry is subject to and serves the overall national strategy. China adheres to the principles of innovation-driven, coordinated, efficient, and peaceful progress based on cooperation and sharing to ensure a high-quality space industry.

Reading Comprehension

Background Information

中国航天事业起始于1956年。中国于1970年4月24日发射第一颗人造地球卫星，是世界上第5个能独立发射人造卫星的国家。中国发展航天事业的宗旨是：探索外太空，扩展对地球和宇宙的认识；和平利用外太空，促进人类文明和社会进步，造福全人类；满足经济建设、科技发展、国家安全和社会进步等方面的需求，提高全民科学素质，维护国家权益，增强综合国力。中国将开启全面建设航天强国新征程。

Critical Thinking

Question One: What's the significance of developing space exploration? What will China develop in outer space?

Question Two: What can ordinary people do for space exploration? What is your expertise or interest? Do you support researching and developing space exploration?

Question Three: How can cosmic exploration benefit mankind? Whether the livelihood economy and aviation development should be balanced or not?

Language Focus

英语句子结构上具有后开放性特点，因此在使用英语表达时应该先将句子的主干提取出来，最后再添上句子的其他附加成分。

句子主干 指的是构成一个完整句子的框架，主要包括几个基本句子成分：主

语、谓语、宾语、表语。

本语篇一共由5个句子构成，它们的句子主干分别是：

☆The industry is a part.

☆Industry has produced a scorecard.

☆China will integrate science, technology and application.

☆Industry is subject to and serves the strategy.

☆China adheres to the principles.

句子附加成分 指的是去除一个完整句子中的主干部分剩余的修饰、补充说明部分，主要包括几个基本句子成分：定语、状语、宾语补足语、主语补足语、同位语、插入语。

本语篇的句子附加成分如下：

★of the country's overall strategy（介词短语作定语）

★the country's overall strategy（country's是名词所有格作定语）

★by the nation's first independent Mars mission（介词短语作状语）

★of a global navigation satellite network and a landmark adventure（介词短语作定语）

★landmark adventure（名词作定语）

★In the next five years（介词短语作状语）

★while adhering to the new development concept（while是连词，放在现在分词短语前，强调动作同时发生）

★of innovation-driven, coordinated, efficient, and peaceful progress（介词短语作定语）

★innovation-driven（名词+过去分词构成复合形容词，作定语）

★high-quality（复合名词作定语）

非谓语动词 是指动词在句子中不作谓语时的形式，因此它不受主语的限制。非谓语动词在英语句子中使用频繁且广泛。它可以在句子中充当除了谓语之外的其他成分，主语、宾语、表语、定语、状语、补语等。非谓语动词分为3大类：

◆动词不定式：to do / to be

◆动名词：doing / being

◆分词，一个是现在分词：doing / being；另一个是过去分词：done / been。

本语篇中非谓语动词的使用：

◇**adhering to** the new development concept，**building** a new development model and **meeting** the requirements of high-quality development 并列现在分词短语作状语

◇innovation-**driven** 名词和过去分词一起构成复合形容词，作定语

◇**based** on cooperation 过去分词短语作定语

◇**sharing** to ensure 动名词短语作介词on的宾语

句子类型 主要包括：简单句、复合句和并列句。在用英文表达时，尽量得体、恰当地交叉使用它们。简单句是指，一个主语或者两个、多个并列主语加上一个谓语或者两个、多个并列谓语构成的句子。复合句是指，一个主句加上一个或者多个从句构成的句子。并列句是指，由并列连词把两个或多个简单句连在一起构成的句子。

本语篇中句子类型的使用：

◎The space industry is a critical part of the country's overall strategy.

简单句：一个主语The space industry，一个系动词is，表语a critical part。

◎China's space industry has produced a remarkable scorecard this year which is characterized by the nation's first independent Mars mission，the completion of a global navigation satellite network and a landmark adventure that retrieved rocks and soil from the moon.

复合句：一个主句China's space industry has produced a remarkable scorecard this year，两个从句which is characterized by...和that retrieved rocks and soil from the moon。

◎In the next five years，China will integrate space science，technology and application while adhering to the new development concept，building a new development model and meeting the requirements of high-quality development.

简单句：一个主语China，一个谓语will integrate。

◎China's space industry is subject to and serves the overall national strategy.

简单句：一个主语China's space industry，两个谓语is subject to和serves。

◎China adheres to the principles of innovation-driven，coordinated，efficient，and peaceful progress based on cooperation and sharing to ensure a high-quality space industry.

简单句：一个主语China，一个谓语adheres to。

主从复合句点拨：无论是主句还是从句，叫作"句"就一定有谓语动词。从句也是句子，判定是什么从句就看该从句在整个复合句中充当什么句子成分。如，定语从句就是该从句在整个复合句中作定语成分。关系代词that在从句中既可用作主语，也可作宾语（在非正式文体中可以省去）；既可指人，又可指物。which在从句中既可作主语，又可作宾语、定语、表语；一般指物（在非正式文体中可以省去）。先行词指物时，关系代词that和which往往可以互换。

构词与常用搭配

critical（*a.*）批判的；关键的：由词根crit（判断，决定）+-ic（……人，……家）名词词尾+形容词词尾-al构成。

常用搭配：a critical moment in our country's history, in a critical condition, develop critical thinking, greatest critical success, be critical to our future, be of critical importance, a critical comment/report

remarkable（*a.*）引人注目的；卓越的：由动词remark（评论；觉察）加上形容词后缀-able构成。

常用搭配：a remarkable achievement/career/talent, make remarkable headway in, with remarkable speed, a remarkable series of gains in technical innovation, remarkable economic results

characterize（*v.*）使具有特点：由词根character（特性，性质）加上动词后缀-ize构成动词。同词根的：character, characteristic。

常用搭配：be characterized by tall modern buildings, characterize the relationship as, characterize one's behavior as, be characterized by humour and biting satire

mission（*n.*）使命；代表团：由词根miss（send送，放出）加上名词后缀-ion构成名词。同词根的：submission, dismiss。

常用搭配：a trade mission to China, a fact-finding mission, a mercy mission to aid homeless refugees, send sb on a diplomatic mission to, a senior member of a diplomatic mission, the first shuttle mission

global（*a.*）全球的；整体的：由名词globe（地球；世界）加形容词后缀-al构成。

常用搭配：calling for a global ban on whaling, take a more global approach to the problem，global issues，a global vision of contemporary societies，the global output of a factory，the dangers of global warming，on a global scale

navigation（*n.*）航行（学）；航海（术）：由动词navigate加上名词后缀-ation构成名词。navigate由词根nav（船）+-ig-（驾驶，引导）+动词词尾-ate构成。同词根的：navy，circumnavigate

常用搭配：navigation systems，an expert in navigation，the right of navigation through international waters，a threat to navigation，an instrument of navigation，a laser navigation device

retrieve（*v.*）取回；恢复：来自古法语。前缀 re-（再，重新）。词源同 trove，contrive。

常用搭配：to retrieve information from the database，to retrieve some of the stolen money，retrieve the situation by apologizing，retrieve the firm from ruin

application（*n.*）申请；运用：由动词apply加名词后缀-ation构成。词根ply（从事；折叠）

常用搭配：have wide application / a wide range of applications in industry，lotion for external application only，strict application of the law，the application of new technology to teaching，a planning / passport application，an application for membership / a loan / a licence，an application form，learn the practical application of the theory

innovation（*n.*）创新；新观念：由表加强意义的前缀 in-加词根 nov（new，新的）加名词后缀-ation构成。同词根的：novel，renovation。

常用搭配：an age of technological innovation，the transformation brought by the technological innovations of the industrial age，promote originality and encourage innovation

coordinated（*a.*）协调的：由动词coordinate（协调；搭配）加上形容词后缀-ed构成。coordinate是由前缀co-（共同）+词根ordin（命令，顺序）+表动词的后缀-ate构成。同词根的：extraordinary，ordinary。

常用搭配：be coordinated with the picture，coordinated troop movements，a coordinated action

cooperation（*n.*）合作；协助：由前缀co-（共同）+词根oper（work工作）+名词后缀-ation构成。同词根的：operation，opera

常用搭配：in cooperation with， closer cooperation between parents and schools， encourage the spirit of voluntary cooperation in its citizens， thank you for your cooperation， attaches great importance to friendly relations and cooperation with

Crossword Puzzle

Across

2. an operation that is assigned by a higher headquarters

3. marked by a tendency to find and call attention to errors and flaws

6. a verbal or written request for assistance or employment or admission to a school

8. unusual or striking

9. the practice of cooperating

11. involving the entire earth； not limited or provincial in scope

Down

1. a creation（a new device or process）resulting from study and experimentation

3. describe or portray the character or the qualities or peculiarities of

4. get or find back； recover the use of

5. operating as a unit

7. the guidance of ships or airplanes from place to place

10. an interconnected system of things or people

Section B　Module Project：Global Issues Discussion

新中国成立73年以来，在华夏大地发生了哪些沧桑巨变？你是否准备好了向世界积极展示中国形象和中国智慧，为构成国际传播矩阵贡献自己的一分力量？

Short Video Project：What great changes have taken place in China？How will you tell the whole world？Could you make them short videos and then post these videos on websites to internationally and proudly spread the marvelous changes？

Section C　Learners' Presentation

China's High-Speed Rail
中国高铁

面对人工智能时代，我国国际传播的未来发展和机遇：我们将运用人工智能新技术开展科技与文化相融合的世界公民社会责任行动，讲好热爱和平保护地球家园、共创人类命运共同体的和平发展故事。运用AI讲好人民幸福生活和民族复兴的中国IP故事，从而消解西方版中国故事对真实、立体的中国形象意义盲区与理解隔阂。我们要积极参与AI聊天机器人的内容生成，助力它的人格成长和伦理建构，通过全人类共同训练和引导，使其爱和平、爱人类、爱地球，使之成为人类永久和平的智能帮手，让中国智慧为开创太平新局面发出时代强音。

Section D   Reflective Assessment

成长档案袋

	Y	N	Achievements
Am I satisfied with my project products?			
Shall I further improve my project products?			
Are my project products popular online?			
Can I take a pride in internationally some marvelous changes in China?			
Have I mastered the vocabulary, sentence patterns and some background information on the great changes in China?			

Keys

Module One
Chinese Scientists

Across

2. coming or happening one after another in a series (successive)
4. feeling a lot of love, respect, and duty towards one's own country (patriotic)
6. extremely enjoyable or exciting (marvelous)
7. to help something to increase, improve, or become more successful (boost)
10. people or groups working together to produce something (collaborative)
11. spending all one's time and effort on something (dedicated)
12. new, original, and advanced; inventing or using new ideas, methods, equipment, etc. (innovative)

Down

1. something is certainly true or is accepted by everyone (undoubtedly)
3. extremely useful (invaluable)
5. a useful or valuable quality (assets)
8. the process of becoming active, successful, or popular again (revival)
9. the fact of achieving or succeeding at things in general (achievement)

Chinese Philosophers

Across

2. bring into conformity with rules or principles or usage; impose regulations (govern)

4. a wise person who is calm and rational; someone who lives a life of reason with equanimity (philosopher)

5. the state of being inactive (inaction)

6. include in scope; include as part of something broader; have as one's sphere or territory (embrace)

9. adhering to moral principles (righteousness)

10. change to the contrary (reverse)

Down

1. able to be compared or worthy of comparison emerge; come out into view, as from concealment (comparable)

3. a person who represents others (representative)

7. violating or tending to violate or offend against (offensive)

8. come out into view, as from concealment (emerge)

Chinese Female Volleyball Athletes

Across

2. strong and able to deal with difficult situations or pain (tough)

4. meaning the same or nearly the same (synonymous)

6. stubbornly unyielding (tenacious)

7. to make a lot of effort to achieve something (striving)

9. generally accepted, recognized or made known or admitted (acknowledged)

10. making people feel enthusiastic or excited about something (inspiring)

12. to try very hard to do something (endeavor)

Down

1. a person trained to compete in sports (athlete)

3. giving courage or confidence or hope (encouraging)

5. to make someone feel determined to do something or enthusiastic about doing (motivating)

8. everywhere or in every situation (universally)

11. an effect, or an influence (impact)

Combating Natural Disasters in China

Across

4. a political theory that the people should own the means of production (collectivism)

7. to show something clearly, especially a feeling, an atitude or a quality (manifest)

8. the act of not allowing yourself to have or do something in order to help other people (self-sacrifice)

9. people in general (humanity)

10. love of country and willingness to sacrifice for it (patriotism)

11. to help something to happen or develop (promote)

12. to do something in order to try to stop something bad from happening or a bad situation from becoming worse (combat)

Down

1. an event that proves a fact (demonstration)

2. having existed for a long time (long-standing)

3. an unexpected event that kills a lot of people or causes a lot of damage (disaster)

5. the quality of being united into one (unity)

6. the phenomenon of vitality and freshness being restored (rejuvenation)

8. support by one person or group of people for another because they share feelings, opinions, aims, etc. (solidarity)

Online Teachers in China

Across

3. to develop gradually, or to cause something or someone to develop gradually (evolve)

4. to give something out to several people, or to spread or supply something (distribute)

9. slowly over a period of time or a distance (gradually)

10. recording or storing information as series of the numbers 1 and 0, to show that a signal is present or absent (digital)

Down

1. to increase or become successful and produce a lot of money very quickly (boom)

2. to be helped by something or to help someone (benefit)

5. having, or being likely to cause, a very close friendship or personal or sexual relationship (intimate)

6. a teacher of a college or university subject (instructor)

7. an opportunity to make your ideas or beliefs known publicly (platform)

8. to result in or discover something, especially proof (produce)

Good Samaritan in China

Across

2. to save somebody or something from a dangerous or harmful situation (rescue)

3. to do something illegal or morally wrong (commit)

6. a period of 10 years (decade)

7. a period of 1000 years (millennium)

10. the choicest or most essential or most vital part of some idea or experience (core)

11. an organization or idea that people support or fight for (cause)

12. your feet slide accidentally and you lose your balance or fall over (slip)

Down

1. towards, onto or on land, having come from an area of water such as the sea or a river (ashore)

4. a person who voluntarily offers help or sympathy in times of trouble (samaritan)

5. the action of deliberately killing yourself (suicide)

8. connected with beliefs and principles about what is right and wrong (ethical)

9. to give something to somebody, especially to show how much they are respected (bestow)

The Westward Relocation of Jiao Tong University

Across

2. all the teachers of a particular university or college (faculty)

5. an official organization or government department that has the power to make decisions (authorities)

6. an action or a service that helps to cause or increase something (contribution)

7, introducing ideas and methods that have never been used before (pioneering)

10. to make something increase, or become better or more successful (boost)

11. behaviour or attitudes that show high moral standards (virtue)

12. the phenomenon of vitality and freshness being restored (rejuvenation)

13. an important official job that a person or group of people is given to do (mission)

Down

1. it is used to describe things that relate to the work done in schools, colleges, and universities (academic)

3. on land beside an ocean (coastal)

4. a state of human society that is very developed and organized (civilization)

8. having fine personal qualities that people admire, such as courage and honesty (noble)

9. the most important or famous (foremost)

Senior Citizens in China

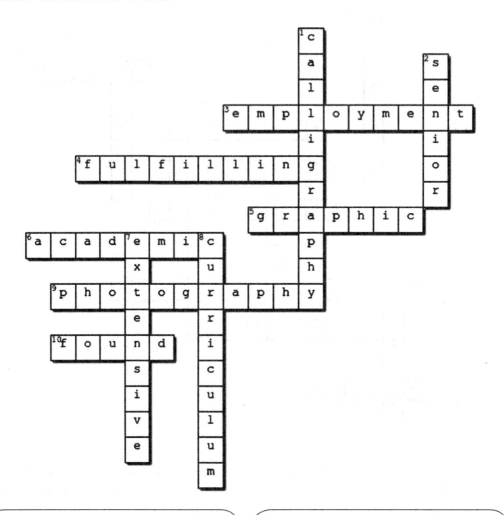

Across

3. the fact of someone being paid to work for a company or an organization (employment)

4. making you feel happy and satisfied (fulfilling)

5. related to drawing or printing (graphic)

6. relating to schools, colleges, and universities, or connected with studying and thinking, not with practical skills (academic)

9. the activity or job of taking photographs or filming (photography)

10. to bring something into existence (found)

Down

1. beautiful writing, often created with a special pen or brush (calligraphy)

2. high or higher in rank (senior)

7. covering a large area; having a great range (extensive)

8. the subjects studied in a school, college, etc. and what each subject includes (curriculum)

The Afforestation Pioneers on Saihanba Highland

The crossword solution grid contains the following answers:

- 1 Down: civilization
- 2 Across: ecological
- 3 Down: miracle
- 4 Down: indescribable
- 5 Down: generation
- 6 Across: dedication
- 7 Down: pioneer
- 8 Across: perch
- 9 Across: afforestation
- 9 Down: artificial
- 10 Across: endure
- 11 Across: adversity

Across

2. concerned about the ecology of a place (ecological)
6. the large amount of time and effort that someone spends on something (dedication)
8. a place for a bird to land or rest on (perch)
9. the conversion of bare or cultivated land into forest (afforestation)
10. to experience and deal with something that is painful or unpleasant, especially without complaining (endure)
11. a difficult or unpleasant situation (adversity)

Down

1. a state of human society that is very developed and organized (civilization)
3. any amazing or wonderful occurrence (miracle)
4. so extreme or unusual it is almost impossible to describe (indescribable)
5. group of people in society who are born and live around the same time; a particular group existing at a particular time (generation)
7. one of the first people to do something important that is later continued and developed by other people (pioneer)
9. created by people; not happening naturally (artificial)

Module Two
The Tiger in Chinese Culture

Across

3. to join together with other people in order to do something as a group (unite)

5. a system by which time is divided into fixed periods, showing the beginning and end of a year (calendar)

8. impressive, making you feel respect and admiration (awe-inspiring)

9. of, involving, caused by, or affecting the moon (lunar)

Down

1. anything that makes it difficult for you to do something (obstacle)

2. very active, determined or full of energy (vigorous)

4. operating with or marked by vigor or effect (energetic)

6. the ability to keep increasing or developing (momentum)

7. a situation that is difficult and unpleasant because you do not have enough money, food, clothes, etc. (hardship)

Couplets in Chinese Culture

Across

4. to find the origin or cause of something (trace)

5. the money, property, etc. that you receive from somebody when they die; the fact of receiving something when somebody dies (inheritance)

6. a series of rulers of a country who all belong to the same family (dynasty)

7. the importance of something, especially when this has an effect on what happens in the future (significance)

Down

1. to be a member of a group of people and act or speak on their behalf at an event, a meeting, etc. (represent)

2. impossible to forget (unforgettable)

3. to fasten or join one thing to another (attach)

Tea Culture

Across

4. a particular part or feature of a situation，an idea，a problem，etc，a way in which it may be considered（aspect）

5. an act of giving something to somebody or doing something for somebody and receiving something in return（exchange）

6. a situation，pattern，etc. containing a lot of different parts that are always changing（kaleldoscope）

10. a quality or characteristic that something has（property）

Down

1. the act of showing something，for example works of art，to the public（exhibition）

2. the effect that somebody/something has on the way a person thinks or behaves or on the way that something. works or develops（influence）

3. a meeting for discussion or training（seminar）

7. to make a lot of people know about something and enjoy it（popularize）

8. the business activity connected with providing accommodation，services and entertainment for people who are visiting a place（tourism）

9. made of many different things or parts that are connected；difficult to understand（complex）

Embroidery Culture

Across

1. to use something, especially fuel, energy or time (consume)

4. a popular way of behaving, doing an activity, etc. (fashion)

6. patterns that are sewn onto cloth using threads of various colours; cloth that is decorated in this way (embroidery)

Down

2. special local product (specialty)

3. belonging to a period of history that is thousands of years in the past (ancient)

5. the size or measurement of something from one end to the other (length)

Traditional Chinese Medicine（TCM）

Across

1. something that is done to cure an illness or injury, or to make somebody look and feel good（treatment）

3. several different sorts of the same thing（variety）

4. in a way that is successful and achieves what you want（effectively）

6. involving a lot of different parts, in a way that is difficult to understand（complicated）

8. not feeling physically relaxed, warm, etc.（uncomfortable）

10. treatment for illness or injury, or the study of this（medicine）

11. relating to or made from herbs（herbal）

Down

2. being part of the beliefs, customs or way of life of a particular group of people, that have not changed for a long time（traditional）

5. a state where things are of equal weight or force（balance）

7. to be one of the causes of something（contribute）

9. illness of people, animals, plants, etc., caused by infection or a failure of health rather than by an accident（disease）

Chinese Winter Solstice Culture

Across

2. the act of drawing spatially closer to something (approach)

6. determine or indicate the place, site, or limits of, as if by an instrument or by a survey (locate)

7. the offering of food, objects or the lives of animals to a higher purpose, in particular divine beings, as an act of propition (sacrifice)

Down

1. a sequence of powerful leaders in the same family (dynasty)

3. half of the terrestrial globe (hemisphere)

4. either of the two times of the year when the sun is at its greatest distance from the celestial equator (solstice)

5. a system of timekeeping that defines the beginning and length and divisions of the year (calendar)

Ethnic Culture

Across

2. a group of people living in a particular local area (community)

3. of many different kinds purposefully arranged but lacking any uniformity (various)

7. giving or be given to each of several people (distribution)

8. to recognize someone and be able to tell who they are (identify)

Down

1. (of political bodies) not controlled by outside forces (autonomous)

4. belonging to times long past (ancient)

5. a branch of applied mathematics concerned with the collection and interpretation of quantitative data and the use of probability (statistics)

6. a group of people who differ racially or politically from a larger group of which it is a part (minority)

Yangtze River Culture

Across

3. a letter or notice sent to a large number of people (circular)

7. the act of making all the people involved in a plan or activity work together in an organized way (coordination)

8. a subject or problem that people are thinking and talking about (issue)

9. to make something stronger or more effective, or to become stronger or more effective (strengthen)

10. features belonging to the culture of a particular society, such as traditions, languages, or buildings, that were created in the past and still have historical importance (heritage)

Down

1. necessary for the success or continued existence of something; extremely important (vital)

2. human society with its well developed social organizations, or the culture and way of life of a society or country at a particular period in time (civilization)

4. to keep something as it is, especially in order to prevent it from decaying or being damaged or destroyed (preserve)

5. the beginning or cause of something (origin)

6. to build something or put together different parts to form something whole (construct)

A Bite of China

Across

2. a collection of things sharing a common attribute （category）

5. of a feature that helps to distinguish a person or thing （distinctive）

Down

1. include or contain; have as a component （incorporate）

3. the practice or manner of preparing food or the food so prepared （cuisine）

4. of concern to or concerning the internal affairs of a nation; of or relating to the home （domestic）

Module Three

Green Development of Yangtze River Economic Belt

Across

2. the act of encouraging something to happen or develop (promotion)

4. to decide which of a group of things are the most important so that you can deal with them first (prioritize)

6. to be made of or formed from something (consist)

8. an important discovery or event that helps to improve a situation or provide an answer to a problem (breakthrough)

9. having positive results (productive)

10. relating to ecology or the environment (ecological)

Down

1. to give something, especially money, in order to provide or achieve something together with other people (contribute)

3. a city or town with its own local government, or the local government itself (municipality)

5. the act or process of returning something to its earlier good condition or position (restoration)

7. able to continue over a period of time (sustainable)

An Economic Structure Facilitating Green, Low-Carbon and Circular Development

Across

4. to include someone or something as an important part (feature)

6. to make something possible or easier (facilitate)

8. shaped like a circle (circular)

9. a level of quality (standard)

10. the way in which the parts of a system or object are arranged or organized, or a system arranged in this way (structure)

Down

1. to ask for something forcefully, in a way that shows that you do not expect to be refused (demand)

2. a chemical element that is an important part of other substances such as coal and oil, as well as being contained in all plants and animals (carbon)

3. working or operating quickly and effectively in an organized way (efficient)

5. how good or bad something is (quality)

7. to make many different things work effectively as a whole (coordinate)

The Beautiful China Initiative

Across

4. continued effort and determination (perseverance)

7. to take part in or become involved in an activity (participate)

8. a small piece or amount of something (bit)

9. to put seeds in or on the ground so that plants will grow (sow)

10. to collect a large number of things over a long period of time (accumulate)

Down

1. whole or complete, with nothing missing (entire)

2. having a lot of green, healthy plants, grass, and trees (lush)

3. the protection of plants and animals, natural areas, and interesting and important structures and buildings, especially from the damaging effects of human activity (conservation)

5. a new plan or process to achieve something or solve a problem (initiative)

6. an attempt to do something (endeavor)

Energy Conservation and Emissions Reduction

Across

2. attempt by employing effort（strive）

7. the preservation and careful management of the environment and of natural resources（conservation）

8. spend extravagantly（consume）

9. the concentration of attention or energy on something（focus）

Down

1. choose and follow；as of theories，ideas，policies，strategies or plans（adopt）

2. happening at a time subsequent to a reference time（subsequently）

3. intentional or planned（intended）

4. the technical aspects of doing something（mechanism）

5. a substance that is emitted or released（emission）

6. injurious to physical or mental health（harmful）

Sustainability and Green Development in Guilin

Across

2. to improve, especially something that was old or outdated (upgrade)

7. formed or united into a whole (integrated)

8. the activity of protecting something from loss or danger (preservation)

9. compatibility in opinion and action (harmony)

10. the quality of arousing interest; being attractive or something that attracts (attraction)

11. characterized by the interdependence of living organisms in an environment (ecological)

Down

1. capable of being sustained (sustainable)

3. the spatial property of being scattered about over an area or volume (distribution)

4. situated in a particular spot or position (located)

5. an economic state of growth with rising profits and full employment (prosperity)

6. change or alter in form, appearance, or nature (transform)

8. assign a priority to (prioritize)

Internet of Vehicles in China

Building a Green Nation

Across

2. serving as an essential component (fundamental)

4. the state of being free from danger or injury (security)

5. the totality of surrounding conditions (environment)

8. characterized by toilsome effort to the point of exhaustion; especially physical effort (arduous)

10. having great material or monetary value especially for use or exchange (valuable)

11. an abstract or general idea inferred or derived from specific instances (concept)

Down

1. a useful or valuable quality (asset)

3. the conversion of bare or cultivated land into forest (afforestation)

4. relating to or concerned with strategy (strategic)

6. follow through or carry out a plan without deviation (adhere)

7. contribute to the progress or growth of (promote)

9. available source of wealth; a new or reserve supply that can be drawn upon when needed (resource)

China's Green Development with Recognition and New Opportunities

Across

2. to happen or make something happen sooner or faster (accelerate)

5. an occasion or situation that makes it possible to do something that you want to do or have to do, or the possibility of doing something (opportunity)

6. extremely fast (blistering)

7. a complete change in the appearance or character of something or someone, especially so that that thing or person is improved (transformation)

9. agreement that something is true or legal (recognition)

10. unusual or special and therefore surprising and worth mentioning (remarkable)

Down

1. to give money or a prize following an official decision (award)

3. something that you contribute or do to help produce or achieve something together with other people, or to help make something successful (contribution)

4. to think or believe something will happen, or someone will arrive (expect)

8. full of hope and confidence, or giving cause for hope and confidence (positive)

Green Infrastructure Boosted

Across

2. to improve or increase something (boost)

5. the total amount that can be contained orproduced, or (especially of a person or organization) the ability to do a particular thing (capacity)

6. the basic systems and services, such as transport and power supplies, that a country or organization uses in order to work effectively (infrastructure)

7. to go or move something forward, or to develop or improve something (advance)

8. working or operating quickly and effectively in an organized way (efficient)

9. waste matter such as water or human urine or solid waste (sewage)

Down

1. showing intelligence, or able to learn and understand things easily (intelligent)

3. to start a company or organization that will continue for a long time (establish)

4. the act of getting rid of something, especially by throwing it away (disposal)

5. complete and including everything that is necessary (comprehensive)

Module Four
Profound Changes in Shenzhen

Across

6. having never happened, been done or been known before (unprecedented)

9. a narrow road in the country (lane)

10. the differences between two things gradually disappear so that it is impossible to separate them (merge)

Down

1. being covered in dots (dotted)

2. relating to or concerned with a city or densely populated area (urban)

3. to be near or around something (surrounding)

4. everything you can see when you look across a large area of land (landscape)

5. the size or extent of something, especially when compared with something else (scale)

7. to be real; to be present in a place or situation (exist)

8. connected with or like the countryside (rural)

Extraordinary Changes of E-commerce in China

<table>
<tr><td colspan="3"></td><td>¹b</td></tr>
</table>

Across

3. the metal or paper medium of exchange that is presently used (currency)

6. beyond what is ordinary or usual; highly unusual or exceptional or remarkable (extraordinary)

8. in an amazing manner; to everyone's surprise (amazingly)

9. call for; to signal to a taxi or a bus, in order to get the driver to stop (hail)

10. made for a particular person or purpose (tailored)

Down

1. very popular with somebody (beloved)

2. the activity of buying and selling goods on the Internet (e-commerce)

4. of or relating to electronics; concerned with or using devices that operate on principles governing the behavior of electrons (electronic)

5. suited to your comfort or purpose or needs (convenient)

7. travel back and forth between two points (shuttle)

Dramatic Changes of Yellow River in China

Across

4. to succeed in dealing with or controlling a problem that has been preventing you from achieving something (overcome)

6. the preservation and careful management of the environment and of natural resources (conservation)

8. new, different and likely to have a great effect (radical)

9. exciting and impressive; thrilling in effect (dramatic)

Down

1. absurd and inappropriate (unreasonable)

2. worthy of being depended on; can be trusted to do something well (reliable)

3. the process of extracting moisture (drying-up)

5. a particular society at a particular time and place (civilization)

7. the place where something originated or was nurtured in its early existence (cradle)

A Huge Shopping Revolution

Across

1. a drastic and far-reaching change in ways of thinking and behaving (revolution)
3. a raised horizontal surface (platform)
5. represent in bodily form (embody)
6. the act of delivering or distributing something as goods or mail (delivery)
7. promise of reimbursement in the case of loss (insurances)

Down

2. power to be effective; the quality of being able to bring about an effect (effectiveness)
4. transactions (sales and purchases) having the objective of supplying commodities (commerce)

China's High-Speed Rail

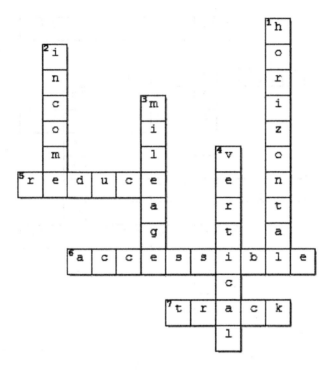

Across

5. lower in grade or rank or force somebody into an undignified situation（reduce）

6. easily obtained（accessible）

7. a pair of parallel rails providing a runway for wheels（track）

Down

1. parallel to or in the plane of the horizon or a base line（horizontal）

2. the financial gain（earned or unearned）accruing over a given period of time（income）

3. distance measured in miles（mileage）

4. at a right angle to another line or plane, or to the earth's surface（vertical）

Rural Revitalization in China

Across

3. a change for the better as a result of correcting abuses (reform)

4. get better (improve)

5. take up and practice as one's own (adopt)

6. move forward, also in the metaphorical sense (advance)

7. the act or process of assigning numbers to phenomena according to a rule (measure)

Down

1. destroy completely, as if down to the roots (eradicate)

2. contribute to the progress or growth of (promote)

8. living in or characteristic of farming or country life (rural)

Mobile Payment in China

Across

5. having no precedent; never having happened, been done or been known before (unprecedented)

7. allow to go; set free or liberate somebody/something (release)

8. free from dirt or substances that may cause disease; hygienic (sanitary)

9. the act of transacting within or between groups (as carrying on commercial activities) (transaction)

Down

1. suited to your comfort or purpose or needs (convenient)

2. a general direction in which something tends to move (trend)

3. examine minutely or intensely (scan)

4. concerned with the ecological effects of altering the environment (environmental)

6. (system of) words, letter, symbols etc. that represent others, used for secret messages or for presenting or recording information (code)

Positive Changes in China's Fitness Industry

Across

3. full of hope and confidence, or giving cause for hope and confidence (positive)

6. very great in amount or level, or extremely good (tremendous)

9. to spend time when you are not working with friends or with other people in order to enjoy yourself (socialize)

10. to see something happen, especially an accident or crime (witness)

Down

1. the condition of being physically strong and healthy (fitness)

2. to broadcast video and sound of an event over the internet as it happens, or to be broadcast in this way (live-stream)

4. to make someone feel energetic or eager (energize)

5. to guess or calculate the cost, size, value, etc. of something (estimate)

7. to copy or move programs or information to a larger computer system or to the internet (upload)

8. an opportunity to make your ideas or beliefs known publicly (platform)

Remarkable Changes of Space Exploration in China

Across

2. an operation that is assigned by a higher headquarters (mission)

3. marked by a tendency to find and call attention to errors and flaws (critical)

6. a verbal or written request for assistance or employment or admission to a school (application)

8. unusual or striking (remarkable)

9. the practice of cooperating (cooperation)

11. involving the entire earth; not limited or provincial in scope (global)

Down

1. a creation (a new device or process) resulting from study and experimentation (innovation)

3. describe or portray the character or the qualities or peculiarities of (characterize)

4. get or find back; recover the use of (retrieve)

5. operating as a unit (coordinated)

7. the guidance of ships or airplanes from place to place (navigation)

10. an interconnected system of things or people (network)

后记

著作此书是一件很辛苦的事。这是一个搭建中外文化交流桥梁的过程，也是一个不停地与国外受众对话的过程，需要字斟句酌，书中每一句话的设计都要尊重其思维习惯，又要揣摩其文化兴趣，还要考虑相应的文化参照物，如此方能完成一句有效的文化交流与沟通。

然而，著作此书，终究是一件很幸福的事。每每夜深人静，浸润在博大精深、绵长厚重的中国文化海洋之中，不停地变换角色，穿梭往返于中外友人之间，穿针引线，想象到此刻他们与我一起达到了被中国文化感动的那种共鸣，这的确是一件很有收获感和幸福感的事。

当行文到此处时，想到快要付梓，不禁长舒一口气，如释重负，心生窃喜。须臾，便又生出丝丝的忐忑。著作此书，诚惶诚恐，如履薄冰，唯恐哪一句表达不尽如人意，致使跨文化交流的桥梁上产生坑坑洼洼的"颠簸"，辜负了读者，辜负了他们传播中国文化的热情。

窃喜与忐忑之余，还想说一些感谢的话。本书编写和出版过程中受到多方的提携襄助，使得著书这样复杂的事情变得如此顺达通畅。

首先，衷心感谢南京大学王海啸教授。王海啸教授是全国大学英语教育领域的杰出领军人物，教育部高等学校大学外语教学指导委员会委员。在此要特别感恩王海啸教授百忙之中审读书稿，亲笔作序，给予盛赞与鼓励。其次，感谢辽宁大学知名学者李玉华和UNIVERISTY OF LEEDS传播学博士EMMA DU，在如何有效推进中国文化国际传播方面给予了本书权威的指导。还有国家一级美术师王仁祥油画大师授权的4幅具有写意油画风格的作品作为本书插画，它们的表现主义和中国写意精神完美结合，起到了助力传播中国文化的作用。同时，真诚感谢AMAR MISSOUM提供本人照片一幅作为图书封面。最后，要感谢沈阳工程学院外语学院、研究生部和科技处，以及万卷出版公司的鼎力相助！

中国文化太过博大精深，著作此书，选取素材的过程是一个艰辛的过程。受制于篇幅所限，一本书无法详尽收纳更多的内容，不得不说这是一件憾事。同时，受制于时间所限，本书距离读者的期许还有很大差距。恳请广大读者不吝指正，您的宝贵意见是我前行的动力。真诚希望与读者一同运用新媒体、新技术助推中国文化走出去，为构建中国文化国际传播矩阵贡献自己的一分力量。

编者

2023年4月

基金项目

本著作是2021年度辽宁省社会科学规划基金项目"提升绿色低碳发展理念的国际传播能力研究"（L21BYY028）的研究成果。